My guess is that you want to fulfill every bit of God's destiny for your life. If I am right, one of the things that is necessary to make it happen is to recognize that you are enthroned with Christ. All too few know this, and even fewer understand how to walk it out. That is why Jeff Jansen's book, *Enthroned*, could not be more timely. More than any other book I know, it draws you into the Throne Room of God and sends you out equipped to advance His Kingdom here on earth in a way that will make a huge difference to you and to those around you! You will love this book!

C. Peter Wagner
(8/15/1930 - 10/21/2016)

In his new book, *Enthroned*, Jeff Jansen shares the reality of our supernatural place in the Kingdom of God as joint heirs with Christ. We are family with God! I believe this book will help all believers to know and understand who they are and the times we are living in before the second coming of Jesus Christ.

Bob Jones
Bob Jones Ministries

This new book, *Enthroned* by Jeff Jansen, will awaken your heart to a fuller understanding of who you are in Christ and inspire you to go higher than you have ever gone before in the glory of God. I highly recommend this book to all.

Bobby Conner
Eagles View Ministries

Brilliant! *Enthroned* is a great addition to the arsenal of weapons available today to help unleash Heaven on earth through the Spirit of Revival. Jeff Jansen is an apostolic voice and present-day revivalist who carries a timely word for the worship, presence, and supernatural moves of the Holy Spirit in the earth today. Excellent!

James W. Goll
President, God Encounters Ministries
Founder, Prayer Storm Ministries and Women on the Frontlines
Best-selling author in the global prayer and prophetic movement

Jeff Jansen has just opened the door for us to walk into a fresh revelation of the privilege our Father has given us to sit Enthroned with Him and decree His will, from Heaven to earth. This book will make you return to the place of prayer with a renewed faith and boldness that comes from the revelation of our true identity in Christ. An amazing must read!

Karen Wheaton
Author, founder of The Ramp

ENTHRONED

Other Destiny Image Books by Jeff Jansen

Furious Sound of Glory

Glory Rising

May be purchased online at Destiny Image

www.destinyimage.com

ENTHRONED

*Manifesting the Power and Glory
of Your Divine Union in Christ*

JEFF JANSEN

DESTINY IMAGE® PUBLISHERS, INC.
P.O. Box 310, Shippensburg, PA 17257-0310
"Promoting Inspired Lives."

This book and all other Destiny Image and Destiny Image Fiction books are available at Christian bookstores and distributors worldwide.
Previously published 2014 by Global Fire Creations.
For more information on foreign distributors, call 717-532-3040.
Or reach us on the Internet: www.destinyimage.com

ISBN 13 TP: 978-0-7684-1943-6
ISBN 13 EBook: 978-0-7684-1944-3
ISBN LP: 978-0-7684-1945-0
ISBN HC: 978-0-7684-1946-7
For Worldwide Distribution, Printed in the U.S.A.
1 2 3 4 5 6 / 21 20 19 18

CONTENTS

FOREWORD

This has been a season of boldly ascending through the door of Heaven. One of the most incredible blessings we can enjoy as followers of Jesus is the right to ascend into the Throne Room. Worship takes us through the steps of ascension into the heavenly realms. The Lord Jesus Christ then mediates our arrival into the Throne Room, where we have the incredible privilege of standing boldly before our holy God. As we ascend, we gain more and more revelation of who He is and what His will is for our lives on earth. Our access is possible because Jesus has paved the way and became the model of ascension for us. In fact, He gives us even greater access than Old Testament believers had, because He has ascended and sits at the right hand of the Father. This book, *Enthroned*, by Jeff Jansen, will help you experience and understand the power of ascension.

When Jesus ascended, He gave gifts to humankind. Most know these gifts as the fivefold ministry gifts. I call them "ascension gifts" that govern earth. Jesus released these gifts to individuals on earth, so that we could maintain the strata. Without us ascending, we can never come into the fullness of the unity of these gifts or exercise the faith that overcomes the evil workings of the enemy within earth. Or put another way, we cannot enter into *enthroned living* and embrace His glory!

When the glory of God comes into our midst, *things change!* The norm is disrupted. I believe going from glory to glory is one of the hardest things we must overcome in Christianity. In this book, Jeff explains "mental *metamorphoo.*" In Ephesians 6:11, the Word of God instructs us to put on the whole armor of God that we might stand against the wiles, or scheming, of the devil.

In the Greek, the word "wiles" is *methodeia* and means "the method or trickery that lies in wait." This is how religious spirits compete with and stop the next move of God's glory on earth. When we do not want to move on and experience what God has for us today, we are tricked into thinking that what we have experienced in the past is good enough. Therefore, the glory of God begins to actually depart from us.

We find an example of this in First Samuel 4. The leadership and the people had fallen into such disarray that the Ark of the Lord was captured in battle. Phinehas' wife said, during her laborious childbirth, *"The glory has departed"* (1 Sam. 4:21).

When we stop moving forward in worship, the awe, glory, and presence of God eventually leaves. This does not happen suddenly. Usually, it starts when we resist change, and the departure progresses over time. I believe we lose our desperation for God. We would rather not change, so we settle for a form of godliness rather than seek God Himself. We have to remember the principle in First Samuel 4. Israel had fallen into disarray because of an ungodly priesthood. This caused the glory of God to depart. However, we see that the presence of God lingered. The Ark of the Covenant of God represented His presence. Eventually, the Ark was captured by the enemy's camp.

Likewise, we have access to the glory and the presence of God; yet because we do not recognize and honor His glory and presence in our midst, He allows Himself to be removed. But part of every believer's spiritual inheritance is to live a "Heaven-on-earth" life. This life is not based on what we have done, but on our intimacy with Christ. In *Enthroned,* Jeff helps every believer gain a fresh perspective of how we are to truly live in the earth realm, and how this postures us to advance the Kingdom of God. Far too many complicate what it takes to live out our heavenly walk, but this book will help you understand that enthroned living is simply living Heaven on earth.

The word "enthroned" means, by implication, to "dwell." Since God has come to enthrone Himself on our praises, the implication in the Hebrew is that God has come to stay or to dwell—even to marry. Where most translations of the Bible use the word "enthroned," the King James Version says that God "inhabits" our praises. The different translations are not at odds with each other; they just express two dimensions of the same Hebrew word. God has chosen Zion—that place of continual praise—as His dwelling place; His resting place forever (see Ps. 132:13). David, by establishing continual praise in the tabernacle on Zion, provided a dwelling place for the Lord.

Today, God is rebuilding the tabernacle and rebuilding Zion in us, His people. Recently, the Lord showed me a plumb line coming down from Heaven. He is realigning His apostolic, prophetic troops on the earth and building a triumphant people who will display the glory of God. We are His dwelling place, His Throne Room. In us and in our praises God comes to dwell and to enthrone Himself. From that dwelling place, that chamber, God is drawing us out into apostolic worship in His larger world, to affect the issues in His Kingdom and bring in the harvest of the earth.

When we enthrone God on our praises, we facilitate the interaction between Heaven and earth. What we see in the Book of Revelation—God enthroned on the praises coming forth on His holy hill, Zion—becomes a reality on earth, with God enthroned on the praises coming forth from the earthly Zion, us.

In Heaven, they knew they were enthroning God on their praises and they knew what would happen when God was enthroned. Today, we know that God is enthroned on our praises, but I don't believe we always understand what that means. Perhaps we have understood that we are enthroning God as the Lord of our own life, but we need to understand that God is taking up His authority over the world from His throne, on our praises. This is apostolic worship, when we enter into God's governmental perspective in our praise.

In contrast, when the demonic powers in the heavens are worshipped by the people on earth, an unholy agreement between Heaven and earth is formed, and a throne of iniquity is established. Just as God is enthroned on the praises of His people, demons are enthroned wherever they are worshipped. Whoever is enthroned has the right and power to rule. This was the problem in Egypt, before the exodus. For Israel coming out of Egypt, it was necessary not just to break the power of the gods of Egypt but also to establish a new order of worship to the Lord. This was God's intent from the beginning. This is why He said, "Let My people go that they might worship Me." The nation could not be established in the Promised Land without the Lord being enthroned over them.

Psalm 94:20 says that a throne of iniquity cannot be joined with God. The two cannot rule at the same time. Where God is enthroned by the praise and worship of His people, a throne of iniquity must fall. As God breaks us free from the powers of demonic forces, we must see that the key to becoming established in freedom is to worship God in a new way. From that worship, a new mindset is developed—both of who we were created to be and who created us. We carry our Creator's DNA. Having His mind enables us to set our minds on things above and move beyond the methods and iniquitous patterns of the enemy; our minds can be transformed and renewed in order to ascend into enthroned living.

This book you are reading has the potential to change your world. What Jeff shares will not only help you understand your authority in Christ, but also how to see Heaven and earth connected in your daily life. We are positioned in the Heavens, but we walk on earth (see Eph. 1–2). When we know our abiding place in the heavenlies, we walk with great confidence and faith. We go to war when the enemy tries to pull us out of that abiding place or block us from ascending to that abiding place in Christ.

Jeff Jansen helps you to not fear the end of an age, but to ascend and let hope and faith arise within you. God has a bright future for His people. Jeff makes you have a hunger for revival. Jesus came preaching and demonstrating the power of the Kingdom. This power has been in the earth over the past 2,000 years. Now, we are in an explosive growth and demonstration of this power.

Whether you adhere to a rapture theology or believe that the Kingdom has fully manifested in the earth, this book will help you understand the need for every generation to ascend, praise, and allow the Lord to be enthroned within them. Be willing to go up on a daily basis and experience the glory of God. As you read through this book, a hunger will arise within you to do just that.

Dr. Chuck D. Pierce
President, Global Spheres Inc.
President, Glory of Zion International
and C. Peter Wagner (8/15/1930 - 10/21/2016)

CHAPTER 1

ENTHRONED LIVING
DEFINED

You must always keep in mind that we were raised together with Him, and He made us to sit with Him in the heavenlies; so representatively, we are seated on the throne with Christ. He is the Head of the body. We are members of that body. So if the Head is exalted, the body is exalted with it. If He has been given all authority, that authority belongs to the Church, His body. It is for the benefit of the Church.

—*E. W. Kenyon*

Of all the subjects and books that could be written to encourage believers in their walk with the Lord Jesus Christ, the subject of Throne Room living is in my opinion one of the most crucial. The reality of enthroned living is that Jesus personally invites us to share with Him in His enthronement at the right hand of the Father right now. This invitation is not only set aside for God's generals or anointed ones, but rather is the privilege, right, and inheritance of every Spirit-filled believer on planet Earth.

15

Cum Christo—or "with Christ"—means we are seated with Christ in the heavenly realm and have the right of privilege to enjoy living from Heaven to earth in the now. We are enthroned! It's true that many of God's children have not accepted the invitation into this reality; however, it does not negate the fact that it is intended for all. The fullness of God's blessings and access into the glorious inheritance of the saints are already ours to enjoy in Christ Jesus and awaiting our full comprehension, acceptance, and appropriation.

Jesus shed His blood on Calvary to open to us the way of life with all the benefits of His Kingdom. The right to sit and rule with Him on His heavenly throne in glory is at the top of that list of benefits. Apostle John, when caught away into the Throne Room and permitted to hear what Jesus said to the seven churches, recorded the following in the Book of Revelation:

Behold, I stand at the door and knock; if anyone hears and listens to and heeds My voice and opens the door, I will come in to him and will eat with him, and he [will eat] with Me (Revelation 3:20).

John saw an invitation being offered from Jesus Himself for us to "open the door to Him." The promise from the Lord is that if we open the door to Him, He will come in and eat with us, and we will eat with Him. The next thing John heard the Lord say:

He who overcomes (is victorious), I will grant him to sit beside Me on My throne, as I Myself overcame (was victorious) and sat down beside My Father on His throne (Revelation 3:21).

John was writing to the church at Laodicea, which was lukewarm and self-centered, and yet Jesus was offering them cooperation with Him onto His throne. Entrance into the company of becoming an "overcomer" was quite clear:

> *Look! I stand at the door and knock. If you hear my voice and open the door, I will come in, and we will share a meal together as friends* (Revelation 3:20 NLT).

And in so doing, we are automatically seated with Christ on His seat of authority that the Father gave Him. As overcomers, we share in the glorious inheritance of Jesus Christ as joint heirs or co-seated ones. We rule with ultimate authority on earth and in the heavenly realm. Sadly, most "Christians" do not believe this reality and pass these truths off as notions of bad theology and grandiose thinking, unknowingly cutting themselves off from access to their inheritance through unbelief. How tragic!

An "enthroned believer" is someone who has overcome the self-centered pull on this life, has opened the door to intimate union and fellowship with the Lord Jesus Christ, and is eating and drinking and deriving life from Jesus Christ alone. If we are zealous and repent and open the door to Jesus Christ through intimate union with Him, we can then join Him on His throne as enthroned ones—as overcomers who enjoy rich fellowship with Him.

Jesus has Opened the Way

Enthroned living is the reality of our supernatural union with God Himself. God created us to live in unbroken union with Him continually. As Spirit-filled believers with our roots in Eden, we should live our lives now as we will live in eternity.

Jesus Christ at great cost opened the way back to Eden and to His throne, which, for every believer, should be a true view of supernatural reality! The blood of Jesus Christ provided not only salvation for humanity, but also for the restoration and reconciliation of the whole of creation (see Col. 1:20). The Lord is looking for His Church to be connected above through union with Him, while keeping its body fixed on the earth below, walking out the Kingdom mandate with power and love. To do this, we must reconnect with the Head (Jesus Christ) and grow up spiritually.

Rather, let our lives lovingly express truth [in all things, speaking truly, dealing truly, living truly]. Enfolded in love, let us grow up in every way and in all things into Him Who is the Head, [even] Christ (the Messiah, the Anointed One) (Ephesians 4:15).

Living in the Benefits of Enthronement

Jesus said the overcomer would be enthroned with Him and enjoy all of the benefits of His victory. John tells us that it's our faith that overcomes the world and that the invitation to become an overcomer is for every believer.

For whatever is born of God is victorious over [overcomes] *the world; and this is the victory that conquers* [has overcome] *the world, even our faith* (1 John 5:4).

As our faith grows, we must take hold of our inheritance in Christ. There are six places in the Book of Revelation where the word "overcomer" is used. The first three places all start with:

He who is able to hear, let him listen to and give heed to what the Spirit says to the assemblies (churches). To him who over-comes... (Revelation 2:7,11,17).

18

The fact that they start with *"He who is able to hear"* clearly indicates that an invitation is being offered to those who will hear, listen, and obey. The following three times the word "overcomer" is used in Revelation 2:26; 3:12; and 3:21 are addressed to *"he who overcomes,"* which indicates that Jesus is talking to a mature group of people who have already made the decision as overcomers. It ends with the invitation from Jesus Himself.

He who overcomes (is victorious), I will grant him to sit with Me on My throne, as I Myself overcame (was victorious) and sat down beside My Father on His throne (Revelation 3:21).

We are to be conformed to the image of God's Son. Since Jesus Christ is an Overcomer, then—at least potentially—so are we as well. The truth is that you may not feel like a victorious overcomer and your present level of spiritual maturity may not reflect it just yet, but if you are a believer, you have the potential to walk as an overcomer in Christ. As your mind is renewed and your faith grows, you are able to respond and enter into this reality. If it weren't possible to experience Throne Room living this side of eternity, Jesus would not have offered it to us. But He did!

We can enjoy the radical reality of supernatural union with Him in the here and now. He has given us power, authority, position, and the right of joint seating with Him now in the heavenly sphere.

He has raised us up together with Him and made us sit down together [giving us joint seating with Him] in the heavenly sphere [by virtue of our being] in Christ Jesus (the Messiah, the Anointed One) (Ephesians 2:6).

We Are Identified with Christ

There is a clear need for us today to understand our identity in Christ. The truth of the matter is, as Spirit-filled believers, we share in all of Christ's accomplishments—including His life, death, burial, resurrection, ascension, and enthronement at the right hand of the Father. Apostle Paul teaches us that we are not only the *beneficiaries* of all Christ has done for us, but that we are in fact *participants* in all that He experienced. The following are seven ways we are identified with Him:

1. We were nailed to the cross and co-crucified with Christ:

We know that our old (unrenewed) self was nailed to the cross with Him in order that [our] body [which is the instrument] of sin might be made ineffective and inactive for evil, that we might no longer be the slaves of sin (Romans 6:6).

I have been crucified with Christ [in Him I have shared His crucifixion]; it is no longer I who live, but Christ (the Messiah) lives in me; and the life I now live in the body I live by faith in (by adherence to and reliance on and complete trust in) the Son of God, Who loved me and gave Himself up for me (Galatians 2:20).

But far be it from me to glory [in anything or anyone] except in the cross of our Lord Jesus Christ (the Messiah) through Whom the world has been crucified to me, and I to the world! (Galatians 6:14)

2. We died with Him:

For the love of Christ controls and urges and impels us, because we are of the opinion and conviction that [if] One died for all, then all died; and He died for all, so that all those who live might live no longer to and for themselves, but for Him Who died and was raised again for their sake (2 Corinthians 5:14-15).

If then you have died with Christ to material ways of looking at things and have escaped from the world's crude and elemental notions and teachings of externalism, why do you live as if you still belong to the world? (Colossians 2:20)

Now if we have died with Christ, we believe that we shall also live with Him (Romans 6:8).

For [as far as this world is concerned] you have died, and your [new, real] life is hidden with Christ in God (Colossians 3:3).

For by the death He died, He died to sin [ending His relation to it] once for all; and the life that He lives, He is living to God [in unbroken fellowship with Him]. Even so consider yourselves also dead to sin and your relation to it broken, but alive to God [living in unbroken fellowship with Him] in Christ Jesus (Romans 6:10-11).

3. We were buried with Him:

We were buried therefore with Him by the baptism into death, so that just as Christ was raised from the dead by the glorious [power] of the Father, so we too might [habitually] live and behave in newness of life (Romans 6:4).

Thus you were circumcised when you were buried with Him in your baptism, in which you were also raised with Him to a new life through your faith in the working of God as displayed when He raised Him up from the dead (Colossians 2:12).

4. We were resurrected and made alive with Him:

And you who were dead in trespasses and in the uncircumcision of your flesh (your sensuality, your sinful carnal nature), [God] brought to life together with [Christ], having [freely] forgiven us all our transgressions (Colossians 2:13).

Even when we were dead by [our own] shortcomings and trespasses, He made us alive together in fellowship and in union with Christ; [He gave us the very life of Christ Himself, the same new life with which He quickened Him, for] it is by grace (His favor and mercy which you did not deserve) that you are saved (delivered from judgment and made partakers of Christ's salvation) (Ephesians 2:5).

5. We have been raised and ascended with Him:

If then you have been raised with Christ [to a new life, thus sharing His resurrection from the dead], aim at and seek the [rich, eternal treasures] that are above, where Christ is, seated at the right hand of God (Colossians 3:1).

And He raised us up together with Him and made us sit down together [giving us joint seating with Him] in the heavenly sphere [by virtue of our being] in Christ Jesus (the Messiah, the Anointed One) (Ephesians 2:6).

6. We are seated with Him at the Father's right hand, sharing His enthronement:

And He raised us up together with Him and made us sit down together [giving us joint seating with Him] in the heavenly sphere [by virtue of our being] in Christ Jesus (the Messiah, the Anointed One) (Ephesians 2:6).

7. We will be revealed with Him when He appears:

When Christ, Who is our life, appears, then you also will appear with Him in [the splendor of His] glory (Colossians 3:4).

For [even the whole] creation (all nature) waits expectantly and longs earnestly for God's sons to be made known [waits for the revealing, the disclosing of their sonship] (Romans 8:19).

The following quotes are taken from E. W. Kenyon's book, *Identification: A Romance in Redemption:*[1]

The teaching of identification is the legal side of our Redemption.

It unveils to us what God did in Christ for us, from the time He went to the Cross, until He sat down on the right hand of the Father. The vital side of Redemption is what the Holy Spirit, through the Word, is doing in us now.

Several times Paul uses the preposition "with" in connection with His Substitutionary teaching.

Galatians 2:20, "I have been crucified WITH Christ."

Then he tells us that "he died WITH Christ," that "he was buried WITH Christ.

…He became one with us in death, that we might be one with Him in life.

There is a two-fold oneness; first His oneness with our sin on the cross; second, our oneness with Him sharing in His glory on the throne.

Ephesians 2:6: And raised us up with him, and made us to sit with him in the heavenly places, in Christ Jesus."

He became as we were, so that we might become as He is.

He died to make us live.

He was made sin to make us Righteous.

He became weak to make us strong.

He suffered shame to give us glory.

He went to hell in order to take us to Heaven.

He was condemned in order to Justify us.

He was made sick in order that healing might be ours.

He was cast out from the presence of God in order to make us welcome there.

We have been identified with Jesus Christ in all He has accomplished for us in life and death and have become the beneficiaries of all of His victories.

Jesus took what I deserved so I could get what He deserved. His triumph is my triumph. His defeat of the devil is my defeat of the devil. His absolute authority over the demonic is also my authority. Most importantly, His freedom to come before the Father is my freedom as well. This divine reality has been freely given to us to experience now, but it must be stepped into by faith.

Christ Is the Head of all Things

The goal of the universe and the culmination of God's purpose is to bring all things under the headship of Christ.

[He planned] for the maturity of the times and the climax of the ages to unify all things and head them up and consummate them in Christ, [both] things in heaven and things on the earth (Ephesians 1:10).

Every tongue will confess and every knee will bow to the sovereignty of the Lord Jesus Christ in both the seen and unseen realms, whether they be thrones, dominions, principalities or powers of good or evil, and all will submit to His ultimate lordship and supreme authority.

Therefore [because He stooped so low] God has highly exalted Him and has freely bestowed on Him the name that is above every name, that in (at) the name of Jesus every knee should (must) bow, in heaven and on earth, and every tongue [frankly and openly] confess and acknowledge that Jesus Christ is Lord, to the glory of God the Father (Philippians 2:9-11).

We are to go forward in His name, extend the rule of His reign and increase His government to the ends of the earth. It is the zeal of the Lord Himself that will make this happen:

*Of the increase of His government and of peace there shall be no end, upon the throne of David and over his kingdom, to establish it and to uphold it with justice and with righteousness from the [latter] time forth, even forevermore. **The zeal of the Lord** of hosts will perform this* (Isaiah 9:7).

Everything that has been created has been done so by Jesus Christ who is the Word of God from the very beginning. John states that all things were made by Him and for Him, and that the world did not accept Him. But to anyone who did accept Him, He gave them the authority, power, privilege, and right to become children of God.

> *He came to that which belonged to Him [to His own—His domain, creation, things, world], and they who were His own did not receive Him and did not welcome Him. But to as many as did receive and welcome Him, He gave the authority (power, privilege, right) to become the children of God, that is, to those who believe in (adhere to, trust in, and rely on) His name* (John 1:11-12).

> *For it was in Him that all things were created, in heaven and on earth, things seen and things unseen, whether thrones, dominions, rulers, or authorities; all things were created and exist through Him [by His service, intervention] and in and for Him. And He Himself existed before all things, and in Him all things consist (cohere, are held together)* (Colossians 1:16-17).

It is the Father's purpose to bring all things back under the lordship of Christ. What we have sometimes failed to see is that we are an important factor in Him accomplishing this purpose. Our enthronement with Him is necessary to fulfill God's plan in its entirety. Christ reigns with all His enemies under His feet. We are the Body of Christ. His feet are our feet, so the enemy is under us as well. Paul said to the church at Ephesus:

> *...He raised Him from the dead and seated Him at His [own] right hand in the heavenly [places], far above all rule and*

26

authority and power and dominion and every name that is named [above every title that can be conferred], not only in this age and in this world, but also in the age and the world which are to come. And He has put all things under His feet and has appointed Him the universal and supreme Head of the church [a headship exercised throughout the church] (Ephesians 1:20-22).

Again…we are the very Body of Christ. His feet are our feet, so you can be sure the enemy is under our feet as well.

Endnote

1. E. W. Kenyon, *Identification: A Romance in Redemption* (Kenyon's Gospel Publishing Society, 2012; 26th printing). http://www.smartcontractingsolutions.com/Identification. pdf; accessed December 19, 2017.

CHAPTER 2

REVELATION UNLOCKS ENTHRONEMENT

You think your mountain is large, the sea at a great distance, your own faith small, well, all this may be true, but you have confidence in that Name even if you have not in your own faith. So, in that great Name command the mountain to go—not in your faith, but in that Name. It will go. It must go! It is not the quantity of faith, but the place where it is centered.

—E. W. Kenyon

We need to keep in mind that revelation is the key to unlock the reality of enthronement in our lives. It's the job of the Holy Spirit to bring us into this revelation by the spirit of wisdom and understanding. He delights in unfolding the true riches of spiritual knowledge and enlightenment that are ours in Christ because He has been given to us to guide us into all truth.

In Him all the treasures of [divine] wisdom (comprehensive insight into the ways and purposes of God) and [all the riches of spiritual] knowledge and enlightenment are stored up and lie hidden (Colossians 2:3).

Now we have not received the spirit [that belongs to] the world, but the [Holy] Spirit Who is from God, [given to us] that we might realize and comprehend and appreciate the gifts [of divine favor and blessing so freely and lavishly] bestowed on us by God (1 Corinthians 2:12).

All that we have in Christ has been freely given to us by the grace of God. He delights for us to enter into His glorious provisions. The Holy Spirit longs to unfold these riches to us and enable us to walk in them. In order to receive the unfolding riches of spiritual knowledge, we must hunger and thirst for more of Christ. Jesus said:

Blessed…are those who hunger and thirst for righteousness (uprightness and right standing with God), for they shall be completely satisfied! (Matthew 5:6)

Revelation Brings Manifestation

A person cannot walk in miracles, signs, and wonders without revelation. Revelation brings the manifestation. The manifestation confirms that the revelation comes from God. People cannot argue with the miracles. They may be able to argue with your doctrine, but they cannot fight miracles!

As Jesus was teaching, the power of the Lord was present with Him to heal:

One of those days as He was teaching, there were Pharisees and teachers of the Law sitting by, who had come from every village and town of Galilee and Judea and from Jerusalem. And the power of the Lord was [present] with Him to heal them (Luke 5:17).

The devil hates revelation because it brings power with it for manifestation and healing. Hosea 4:6 says that God's people are destroyed for *"lack of knowledge."* Without revelation knowledge, there is no empowerment.

Revelation Knowledge

I don't think anyone really understands just exactly what Adam experienced when he fell from the glory of God. With the Fall, Adam traded the mind of Christ for the mind of reason. He went from eating of the Tree of Life to eating from the tree of self-recognition.

Common sense wants you to reason, but faith wants you to simply believe and act!

Our intellect has problems with anything that cannot be explained. Not all substance is visible to the naked eye. Hebrews 11:3 tells us that the world we can see with our natural eyes was created by the world that we cannot physically see.

Common sense bases reality on what we can detect with our five natural senses, but this type of thinking by itself is dangerous and incomplete.

God is Spirit, and He is looking for the people who will manifest Heaven on the earth. The society we live in is limited by what it can detect in the physical world. Anything outside of this is inconceivable. The only thing that can take you past your intellect is revelation knowledge. Jesus said:

To you has been entrusted the mystery of the kingdom of God [that is, the secret counsels of God which are hidden from the ungodly]; but for those outside [of our circle] everything becomes a parable (Mark 4:11).

Revelation knowledge is the only thing that can bring us to the place of seeing the unseen realm. The natural mind and intellect can't do it. They are two completely different components altogether. We need the mind of Christ!

Common sense says the physical realm is the boundary by which we are to define reality, and anything beyond that, it cannot accept or believe. But the enthroned believer determines reality based upon the Word of God and the revelation knowledge.

The Holy Spirit must reveal things to us for them to become fruitful in our lives. It's important that we spend time quietly meditating, giving the Holy Spirit time to unveil spiritual truths to us. One verse illuminated by the light of the Holy Spirit will bring the power of transformation in our lives that years of study and meditation cannot.

Christ Is Now Enthroned

We must always remember that we have become the beneficiaries of all of His victories, as He is enthroned at the right hand of the Father *now*. These divine realities have been freely given to us to experience in the now by the grace of God. The early church preached Christ as risen from the dead and enthroned at the Father's right hand. Although they came to understand that He died for their sins, forgiveness of sins was not the emphasis in their preaching. Forgiveness was a benefit of the fact that Jesus had overcome death and opened up to us a new and living way into the Heavens through the veil of His flesh.

By this fresh (new) and living way which He initiated and dedicated and opened for us through the separating curtain (veil of the Holy of Holies), that is, through His flesh (Hebrews 10:20).

Therefore if any person is [ingrafted] in Christ (the Messiah) he is a new creation (a new creature altogether); the old [previous moral and spiritual condition] has passed away. Behold, the fresh and new has come! (2 Corinthians 5:17)

God brought forth a new creation through Christ Jesus and gave fallen humanity His righteousness.

He saved us, not because of any works of righteousness that we had done, but because of His own mercy, by [the] cleansing [bath] of the new birth (regeneration) and renewing of the Holy Spirit (Titus 3:5).

Christ NOW has all authority in Heaven and on earth and does not leave any place for the demonic realm. The devil may seek to maintain his former authority, but he has been dethroned. First Corinthians 2:6 says:

...the leaders and rulers of this age, who are being brought to nothing and are doomed to pass away.

The Church is waking up to the fact that satan has been dethroned, and it is our job to enforce his defeat. We cannot afford to entertain a doctrine that empowers a disempowered devil. Jesus has all authority and has delegated it to us. As joint heirs enthroned with Him, we are to go forward in His name and destroy the works of darkness, just as He did.

[But] he who commits sin [who practices evildoing] is of the devil [takes his character from the evil one], for the devil has sinned (violated the divine law) from the beginning. The reason the Son of God was made manifest (visible) was to undo (destroy, loosen, and dissolve) the works the devil [has done] (1 John 3:8).

Beholding His Death

Or have you forgotten that when we were joined with Christ Jesus in baptism, we joined him in his death? **For we died and were buried with Christ** *by baptism…* (Romans 6:3-4 NLT).

Christ died for our sins and was raised for our justification. May we never stop appreciating what an awesome price Jesus paid to redeem us as He suffered in spirit, soul, and body. His suffering was far greater than anyone has ever suffered. He did it because He loves us.

…He, for the joy [of obtaining the prize] that was set before Him, endured the cross, despising and ignoring the shame, and is now seated at the right hand of the throne of God (Hebrews 12:2).

He endured the cross for the joy set before Him—and that joy was us. His joy was seeing you and me in fellowship with His Father, fulfilling the Father's original intention for humankind. His death secures our forgiveness and place as enthroned with Him.

Question: Are we worthy of the death of Jesus on the cross?

God seems to think so. He is a good investor! He didn't just take His only Son and trade Him for what the Father would consider as trash. Apparently, God saw that you were worth the death of Jesus and have equal the value and worth as His Son!

Beholding His Resurrection

Knowing already that Christ having once then been raised out of the dead ever no more dies; death no more ever lords it over Him (Romans 6:9).

Paul states that the Spirit-filled believer should already fully and completely know that Christ's resurrection is an eternal resurrection. Death will not have any dominion over Him—ever. We were once then "co-quickened" with Christ, "co-raised" in Christ, and "co-seated in the heavenlies" in Christ (see Eph. 2:5-6 Expositor's Greek Testament[1]).

We must remember that not only was Christ crucified for us, but we were crucified with Him and share in His death and resurrection from the dead.

We must see ourselves as those who are dead to the power of sin, because we are alive to God in Christ. We must understand that we are already dead to the power of sin and have been raised with Christ with the dominion of sin broken over us.

For sin shall not [any longer] exert dominion over you, since now you are not under Law [as slaves], but under grace [as subjects of God's favor and mercy] (Romans 6:14).

We have come into our rich inheritance in grace. Grace is more than unmerited favor. Grace is God's divine enablement and willingness to use His power and ability on our behalf—even though we don't deserve it.

When we finally realize that we are literally new creatures in Christ and that we have been enthroned with Him at the Father's right hand, there comes an inward flow of the Holy Spirit that begins to bubble up and flow throughout all our thoughts and actions.

Raised to Live above Sin

As we identify with His resurrection, we begin to take hold of the reality that we have been raised with Christ to live above sin. We declare and decree that sin's dominion is broken over us and we will no longer submit to its enticement. Whoever the Son sets free is free indeed.

> *Which He exerted in Christ when He raised Him from the dead and seated Him* [enthroned] *at His [own] right hand in the heavenly [places], far above all rule and authority and power and dominion and every name that is named [above every title that can be conferred], not only in this age and in this world, but also in the age and the world which are to come* (Ephesians 1:20-21).

Jesus is enthroned far above every principality, ruling force, power, and sovereignty. His name is a higher authority than all other names. Eventually, every knee will bow and every tongue confess His lordship.

His accomplishments are also ours. His resurrection was our resurrection. His enthroning was our enthroning. When all evil forces were put under His feet, they were just as much put under ours. As Christ's joint heirs, we inherit all that He deserves. We reign with Him.

> *For if by the transgression of the one, death reigned through the one, much more those who receive the abundance of grace and of the gift of righteousness will reign in life through the One, Jesus Christ* (Romans 5:17 NASB).

He is the one true heavenly King who lives in the many kings on the earth.

–Jeff Jansen

He is the King of many kings—that's you and me—and kings reign. We have been called to share the reign of Christ. We are predestined to be conformed to the image of God's Son. He is the Firstborn of many brought to glory. Now observe what Christ is expecting while He sits enthroned at the Father's right hand:

But He, having offered one sacrifice for sins for all time, sat down at the right hand of God, waiting from that time onward until His enemies be made a footstool for His feet (Hebrews 10:12-13 NASB).

Jesus is waiting and expecting the Father—through His Body, us—to subdue all His enemies under His feet. The Father will make His enemies a footstool. Satan is portrayed as the footstool of the Body of Christ. Here we see satan's absolute submission to Christ, and therefore, to His Body.

Endnote

1. Expositor's Greek Testament, edited by Rev. W. Robertson Nicoll, MA, LLD, Editor of "The Expositor," "The Expositor's Bible" etc. Volume I-V. New York: George H. Doran Company.

CHAPTER 3

THE HIDDEN WISDOM OF
THRONE ROOM LIVING

You are identified with Christ in all He is, was, or will be. Your enemy may be stubborn and resist you, but your will is set—you are going to win, and you literally charge on the enemy in that all-conquering name of Jesus Christ. The enemy may stand for a time, but he must yield.

—*E. W. Kenyon*

But we speak God's wisdom in a mystery, the hidden wisdom which God predestined before the ages to our glory; the wisdom which none of the rulers of this age has understood; for if they had understood it they would not have crucified the Lord of glory; but just as it is written, "Things which eye has not seen and ear has not heard, and which have not entered the heart of man, all that God has prepared for those who love Him." For to us God revealed them through the Spirit; for the Spirit searches all things, even the depths of God (1 Corinthians 2:7-10 NASB).

This hidden wisdom has been hidden not *from* us, but *for* us. It was hidden so it could be revealed to us for our glory. The Holy Spirit has been given to us to accomplish the task of continually unveiling these riches to us. He delights to bring us into these heavenly realities. The Father has given Him to us so we can know the riches freely given to us by our God. The apostle Paul told us that things are temporarily hidden only as a means to revelation, and that we are to be careful as to what we set our attention upon.

> *[Things are hidden temporarily only as a means to revelation.]*
> *For there is nothing hidden except to be revealed, nor is any-*
> *thing [temporarily] kept secret except in order that it may be*
> *made known. If any man has ears to hear, let him be listening*
> *and let him perceive and comprehend. And He said to them,*
> *Be careful what you are hearing. The measure [of thought and*
> *study] you give [to the truth you hear] will be the measure*
> *[of virtue and knowledge] that comes back to you—and more*
> *[besides] will be given to you who hear* (Mark 4:22-24).

Paul said that the measure of thought and study you give, even to the truth you hear, will be the measure of virtue and knowledge that comes back to you. Paul also encouraged us to set our attention above:

> *If then you have been raised with Christ [to a new life, sharing*
> *His resurrection from the dead], aim at and seek the [rich, eternal*
> *treasures] that are above, where Christ is, seated at the right hand*
> *of God. And set your minds and keep them set on what is above*
> *(the higher things), not on the things that are on the earth. For*
> *[as far as this world is concerned] you have died, and your [new,*
> *real] life is hidden with Christ in God* (Colossians 3:1-3).

We are to keep our focus on living from above. If we keep our focus on even the good things in the lower realm, Paul said that this would be the degree of *virtue* (power) and *revelation* (knowledge) that would come back to us. When our attention is set on Throne Room living, everything that is accessible in that realm will come back to us in full measure. Paul strongly encourages us to keep in the center of our thoughts the reality that:

you have been raised with Christ [to a new life, thus sharing His resurrection from the dead], aim at and seek the [rich, eternal treasures] that are above, where Christ is, seated at the right hand of God (Colossians 1:2).

Past, Present, and Future Mantles

Several years ago while waiting on the Lord, I was taken into a heavenly encounter that impacted my life greatly and caused me to see the reality of my destiny and rise up into it. In this encounter, the Lord came to me and took me by the hand like a little child and led me into what looked like a locker room in Heaven.

As I was standing in this place, I saw what looked to be shaker pegs extending all around the room. Hanging on the pegs were white garments, robes. As I continued to look into the vision, I saw names written above each of the robes. I saw the names of Elijah, Samuel, Jeremiah, Elisha, John Wesley, Charles Finney, Maria Woodworth Etter, and many more. This locker room was in fact a cloak room, or a room of mantles from past revivalists and prophets.

Then I heard the Lord say, "Choose one and I will give it to you." I looked at the mantles hanging in this room with the names above each, and I was seriously considering taking Enoch's mantle, but when I opened my mouth to speak I replied, "Oh Lord, You know which one I should take." In communicating this encounter later to Bob Jones, he said, "Boy that was the best answer you could have given the Lord. You let Him pick for you."

Immediately in the vision the Lord was standing in front of me, and I had a mortar and pestle in my hand used by pharmacists for grinding medicine. The Lord handed me three pills and told me to "grind them." As I ground the three pills, the Lord said, "These three pills are the past, present, and future mantles."

The Lord was offering this hidden wisdom to not only me, but to those who share the entitlement with Him to His throne. All mantles—past, present, and future—are being poured out upon a glory generation of enthroned believers in preparation for a great harvest of souls before the second coming of the Lord Jesus Christ.

The Need for Spiritual Sight

This generation needs to see a demonstration of power and glory. When resurrection power lives in you, the world around you should change. God is pouring out His glory upon a company of overcomers who share enthronement with Him. There is an invitation for us to come into intimate union with the Lord Jesus Christ that will lift us into the glory of His presence where we can share in His inheritance with Him.

But we cannot walk in what we do not know. Paul's desire for the Ephesians was that the Father would give them a:

spirit of wisdom and revelation [of insight into mysteries and secrets] in the [deep and intimate] in the knowledge of Him, by having the eyes of your heart flooded with light so that you can know... (Ephesians 1:17-18).

Paul tells the Corinthians that, in Christ, the veil that covered the Jews when they read the Scriptures is removed. This is how the new covenant believer reads the Word.

And all of us, as with unveiled face, [because we] continued to behold [in the Word of God] as in a mirror the glory of the Lord, are constantly being transfigured into His very own image in ever increasing splendor from one degree of glory to another; [for this comes] from the Lord [Who is] the Spirit (2 Corinthians 3:18).

As we gaze into the Word with the help of the Holy Spirit, we see the glory of the Lord revealed and become transformed. This unveiling of the glory of the Lord causes us to see that we are enthroned with Him at the Father's right hand, far above all powers in this Age and the Age to come.

Our Enthronement with Him

As we come to appreciate the total victory of His resurrection, we realize the utter defeat of the kingdom of darkness. Paul describes it like this:

Which He exerted in Christ when He raised Him from the dead and seated Him at His [own] right hand in the heavenly [places], far above all rule and authority and power and dominion and every name that is named [above every title that can be conferred], not only in this age and in this world, but also in the age and the world which are to come. And He has put all things under His feet and has appointed Him the universal and supreme Head of the church [a headship exercised throughout the church] (Ephesians 1:20-22).

Jesus was raised far above all principality and power, might and dominion. He was given all authority in Heaven and on earth. The Church is just coming to understand that He has all authority in the earth *now*. Darkness is completely inferior to light.

Most of the Church has too big of a devil. We need a fresh perspective. Every manifestation of evil power is an exercise of illegitimate authority. Jesus has put to an open shame all principalities and powers, demonstrated by the Father raising His Son from the dead and seating Him at His own right hand in the heavenly realm:

> *Far above all rule and authority and power and dominion and every name that is named [above every title that can be conferred], not only in this age and in this world, but also in the age and the world which are to come. And He has put all things under His feet and has appointed Him the universal and supreme Head of the church [a headship exercised throughout the church]* (Ephesians 2:21-22).

Devils have no right to reign on earth at all. The Body of Christ has final authority, and many are beginning to take hold of it. Paul proceeds in the Book of Ephesians to show the relationship between what happened to Christ in His resurrection and what happened to us:

> *Even when we were dead in trespasses, made us alive together with Christ (by grace you have been saved), and raised us up together, and made us sit together in the heavenly places in Christ Jesus* (Ephesians 2:5-6 NKJV).

Together, with Christ Jesus and in Him, God raised us up and enthroned us in the heavenly realm.

The Father enthroned us together with Christ. When He raised Christ, He raised us as well. We can only receive and understand these realities by revelation. Our minds cannot figure them out logically, but our recreated spirits can. We must take hold and embrace these realities.

Becoming a Throne of Honor and Glory

Most believers are all too familiar with the Scripture verse Isaiah 22:22 and have heard it used in many different situations:

And the key of the house of David I will lay upon his shoulder; he shall open and no one shall shut, he shall shut and no one shall open (Isaiah 22:22).

But read on and see what the next verse says:

*And I will **fasten him like a peg** or nail in a firm place; and he will become a throne of honor and glory to his father's house* (Isaiah 22:23).

Isaiah saw a company of believers who would be like a peg or a nail in a firm place on which someone would hang a cloak or a mantle. But there is something more interesting stated here. It says:

*...and he will become a **throne of honor and glory** to his father's house* (Isaiah 22:23).

The Scripture says that this individual will become a *"throne of honor and glory."* Who will become a throne of honor and glory? The one whom the key of the house of David rests upon. This individual will become a supernatural gateway for all of Heaven to flow through. Even more than that, it says that this person will become a *throne*. Not only are we seated with Jesus on His throne, but we actually become a throne *"on earth as it is in heaven"* that Christ will reveal His Kingdom through. Try preaching this in some churches! Nonetheless, it is true.

> *But You are holy, O You Who dwell in [the holy place where] the praises of Israel [are offered]* (Psalm 22:3).

The throne of God flows through the praises of His people. What does that look like? Wherever the throne of God is, the King is. Wherever the King is, there is a Kingdom. Wherever the Kingdom is, the angels are—and all of the unlimited resources and currency that Kingdom provides. Our mandate is simple: raise up a generation who can openly display the raw power of God.

When we are connected with Heaven, we become a gateway through which the supernatural can manifest. Heaven moves up and down upon us, releasing the miraculous with our cooperation. It is abnormal for a Christian to not have an appetite for the impossible. It has been written into our spiritual DNA to hunger for the impossibilities around us to bow at the name of Jesus.

The best thing we can be is ourselves, with God moving all over us. The world is looking for us to be signs and wonders to them.

Becoming a Supernatural Gateway of Light

It's important for us to understand what it means to become a gateway of the supernatural realm. The life of Jesus was filled with extraordinary events that reach far beyond what we would call the norm of the day. The disciples also moved in the *exousia* power that flowed from the mantle of the Spirit of the Lord that rested on Jesus' life as He demonstrated to them what it meant to become a gateway in both the natural and spiritual mind.

In Matthew 16:13-17, Jesus asked His disciples:

Who do people say that the Son of Man is? And they answered, Some say John the Baptist; others say Elijah; and others Jeremiah or one of the prophets. He said to them, But who do you [yourselves] say that I am? Simon Peter replied, You are the Christ, the Son of the living God.

Jesus told Peter:

Blessed (happy, fortunate, and to be envied) are you, Simon Bar-Jonah. For flesh and blood [men] have not revealed this to you, but My Father Who is in heaven.

Four verses later, Peter has another revelation after Jesus told them plainly that He would have to go to the cross.

Then Peter took Him aside to speak to Him privately and began to reprove and charge Him sharply, saying, God forbid, Lord! This must never happen to You!

But Jesus turned away from Peter and said to him, Get behind Me, Satan! You are in My way [an offense and a hindrance and a snare to Me]; for you are minding what partakes not of the nature and quality of God, but of men (Matthew 16:22-23).

Peter moved from being a gateway of revelation from the Father in one moment to becoming a gateway of darkness the next, to which the Lord said to him, *"get behind Me, Satan!"* How could this be? From Holy Spirit revelation to satan in less than 60 seconds!

In truth, we all reveal one of two minds, either the natural mind or the mind of the Spirit. Jesus is our great example. He is the firstborn among many. He is in complete union with the Father at all times. As a result, He turned water into wine, had Peter pull a coin out of a fish's mouth, multiplied five loaves of bread and two small fish to feed more than five thousand men, women, and children, walked on water, spoke to fig trees and stormy seas that obeyed Him, and demons acknowledged Him and ran from His presence. The list of supernatural events is so numerous it cannot be recorded. These testimonies were given to us as examples so we would know with certainty what is available and rightfully ours to walk in when rightly connected with God.

Jesus plainly tells us:

I assure you, and most solemnly I tell you, if anyone steadfastly believes in Me, he will himself be able to do the things that I do; and he will do even greater things than these, because I go to the Father (John 14:12).

We Are One Spirit with Him

What does it look like to have the Kingdom of God flowing in and through you, and constantly surrounding you? What does it look like to become a *"throne of honor?"* What does it look like to be united with the Lord as one Spirit with Him? Paul says:

But the person who is united to the Lord becomes one spirit with Him (1 Corinthians 6:17).

Think about that: we are one with the Lord. What type of human being does that actually make you? It makes you a *God-like one* on the earth. You become a *gateway of light* on the earth. Everything in the spirit world sees you. Angels, as well as demons, know who you are. They see the light of God flowing through your spirit as a supernatural highway of the Kingdom of God. We become a throne, and there is One who sits on that throne. Do you get it? Jesus isn't kidding when He says:

If a person [really] loves Me, he will keep My word [obey My teaching]; and My Father will love him, and We will come to him and make Our home (abode, special dwelling place) with him (John 14:23).

Throne Room Thoughts Shape Our World

Our thoughts are actually prayers; they are living and powerful. When our thoughts are connected to the throne of God, they have the ability to create substance in our lives. Enthroned thoughts become the gate to the supernatural realm as desire mixes with the heart.

When I meditate on the Word of God, my thoughts are connected via my enthronement with the Lord, and revelation begins to flow in and through me. When this happens, my whole being seems to flood with light. And not only light, but flood with the tranquil peace of the life of God. My emotions, and the revelation that come from God's mind, are planted deep in the soil of my spirit. It's in this place that the power to create and birth is present.

Revelation that comes from being enthroned with the Lord is not abstract; it creates life deep inside us. When revelation is received, a divine seed is planted. Conception has taken place. And with cultivation, that revelation will bring to birth a manifestation in our life.

This is the process of creation! As a person thinks, so will he become.

Throne Thoughts Create Life

Jesus goes on to reveal the power of your thoughts to create life:

> *For this reason I am telling you, whatever you ask for in prayer,*
> *believe (trust and be confident) that it is granted to you, and*
> *you will [get it]* (Mark 11:24).

Desire is a very powerful emotion. Jesus said desire, believe, speak, and you will have. Our thoughts are not simply abstract thoughts that nobody hears. They are the seeds of desire that produce substance and chart the course of our present and future life. If thoughts are seeds, then we need to understand how they are planted.

When your thoughts connect with desire in the emotions, a power is released. If you can hold your thoughts until they are connected with your emotions or desire, they will become a power—a life and a light. This is the principle of *the power of agreement*. Jesus says:

> *Again, truly I tell you that if two of you on earth agree about*
> *anything they ask for, it will be done for them by my Father in*
> *heaven* (Matthew 18:19 NIV).

We can birth the will of Heaven on earth as enthroned new creations in Christ.

The Power of Union

When your emotions agree with your thinking, it shall be done: that's the power of union. As I wrote about in my book, *Glory Rising*, the Creation Law of Reproduction is a spiritual law that cannot be stopped. Take, for example, the force of fear. Fear is just a thought until it connects with your emotions. You may hear a noise outside your home at night. For a moment your mind is flooded with thoughts about what that noise could be, giving you an adrenalin rush of emotion that produces fear. This thought fills your entire being with its life force and creates the environment of fear and even terror. Thoughts that connect with our emotions become a very strong power.

The Church has taught for years that emotions are not important. I say to you that your emotions and your thought life are the creative side of you. Your emotions are essential for everything to happen. Miracles are released through our emotions. Jesus was moved with compassion. Compassion released miracles—even the raising of the dead.

The power and glory of God in the anointing are released through the gateway of human affection. We have to feel what we do. When our thinking connects with the feeling of what we do, the seed is planted by desire. A power is released. It's the law of union where two things (or people) come into agreement.

Then the evil desire, when it has conceived, gives birth to sin, and sin, when it is fully matured, brings forth death (James 1:15).

When evil desire is conceived by lust (emotion) and thought, the two, coming together, form a creative power bond of agreement that brings forth sin. This phrase *"brings forth"* is the same as the plant that comes from the seed. It is the process of the Creation Law of Reproduction at work. Your thoughts manifest in the natural.

CHAPTER 4

YOU ARE A NEW
CREATION REALITY

He was God manifest in the flesh in His earth walk, and He was God in the Spirit in His Substitutionary sacrifice. At God's right hand He has a glorified body and is Head of the New Creation. You will find that He did a perfect work for us, and the Spirit through the Word does a perfect work in us, as Jesus is today at the right hand of the Father, doing a perfect work for us.

—*E. W. Kenyon*

As the Spirit of the Father unveils to us our high calling, it creates within us a cry for a greater reality and participation with Him. A divine longing sets in when we hunger to live in all that He has provided for us in Christ. As we taste the realities of rebirth, we cease from our striving and begin to rest in Him.

The goodness of God claims the devotion of our hearts, and we cannot help but deepen our surrender to Him. As we see the magnitude of God's love for us, we are taken captive by a desire to know Him intimately. The Holy Spirit draws us to come into friendship with Christ. When Peter described the resurrection of Christ, he quoted Psalm 16.

> *You will show me the path of life; in Your presence is fullness of joy, at Your right hand are pleasures forevermore* (Psalm 16:11).

In His presence or, literally, before His face, there is fullness of joy. Jesus opened a new and living way for us to come back into the presence of God and is a forerunner for all humanity to return to fellowship with the Father.

> *For You will not leave my soul in Hades, nor will You allow Your Holy One to see corruption. You have made known to me the ways of life; You will make me full of joy in Your presence* (Acts 2:27-28 NKJV).

"*You will make me full of joy in Your presence.*" We share this reality with Him. Our Father will make us full of joy in His presence as well! As we grasp this reality, we enter into the rest that Jesus is now enjoying. So rest!

You Are a *Kainos*—New Creation

> *Therefore, if anyone is in Christ, he is a new creation; old things have passed away; behold, all things have become new* (2 Corinthians 5:17 NKJV).

As Christians, we are altogether new and enjoy a new life in a new world. Christians are set free not only from sin and its effects, but are also set free from themselves. The place where we walk when we become Christians is a supernatural place that lifts us out of the old condition and into a divine place of being. We are raised into the human condition that God intended for us when He created us—a people created in His image.

No longer under the enemy and sin, we discover the reason why God created us. The Word of God reveals to us a life that is no longer stuck in the cycle of living in a fallen condition, but as new-creation Christians, we are now free to explore the reality of an eternal life of happiness and holiness in the presence of the Lord.

The Gospel declares that we are *"new creatures"* in Christ! There are two Greek words used in the New Testament for the word "new." The first is *neos*, which means, new of the same kind, the same quality, or the same order.

The second Greek word is *kainos*. The definition of *kainos* is new as to form quality, of a different nature from what is contrasted as old.

If something is *kainos*, it is superior to what it succeeds. Let's examine Second Corinthians 5:17 from several different Bible translations:

> *Therefore, if anyone is in union with Christ, he is a new being* (Twentieth Century New Testament).

> *For if a man is in Christ he becomes a new person altogether* (Phillips).

> *When anyone is united to Christ, there is a new world* (New English Bible).

We are not the same inferior and old-natured humans we once were. We are new! We are *kainos* new! We are new in quality and in kind, and superior to what we were in the old condition.

The Scripture goes on to say, in the next verse, that the old being or person we were before we came to Christ has also been made extinct! Let's examine several different Bible versions of Second Corinthians 5:18:

His old being has passed away (Conybeare).

His old life has disappeared, everything has become new about him (Knox).

The past is finished and gone, everything has become fresh and new (Phillips).

The old order has gone, and a new order has already begun (New English Bible).

The Old *Arkhayos* Is Gone

The old order is gone and everything is new. The Greek word for "old" is *arkhayos*, which is defined as the original or primeval. How amazing! Christ has destroyed our corrupted human side and has created a new person altogether in Him. The old person or old condition has been made completely extinct.

The *new person* is what believers are in Christ. We are completely new when we were crucified and raised with Christ. In this *kainos* event, a whole new reality opens up to us. We are in a new, divinely lifted condition of enthronement with Christ, living in unbroken union with God. Now that's the Good News of the Gospel!

We Have a New Nature

It's important for us to understand that every believer struggling with temptation and the flesh nature has been crucified with Christ

56

and that satan is a defeated foe. The law is powerless to help. Let me ask you some questions:

Question: As a new creation in Christ, have you ever wondered what it was that you were made into? If we have been made into something new, what is that new thing?

Question: If you have a new nature, how different are you from what you were? Do you realize that at this very moment you are the righteousness of God in Christ Jesus?

> *For if because of one man's trespass (lapse, offense) death reigned through that one, much more surely will those who receive [God's] overflowing grace (unmerited favor) and the free gift of righteousness [putting them into right standing with Himself] reign as kings in life through the one Man Jesus Christ (the Messiah, the Anointed One)* (Romans 5:17).

> *But it is from Him that you have your life in Christ Jesus, Whom God made our Wisdom from God, [revealed to us a knowledge of the divine plan of salvation previously hidden, manifesting itself as] our Righteousness [thus making us upright and putting us in right standing with God], and our Consecration [making us pure and holy], and our Redemption [providing our ransom from eternal penalty for sin]* (1 Corinthians 1:30).

> *For by a single offering He has forever completely cleansed and perfected those who are consecrated and made holy* (Hebrews 10:14).

> *Live as children of obedience [to God]; do not conform yourselves to the evil desires [that governed you] in your former ignorance [when you did not know the requirements of the Gospel]. But as the One Who called you is holy, you yourselves also be holy in all*

your conduct and manner of living. For it is written, You shall be holy, for I am holy (1 Peter 1:14-16).

And such some of you were [once]. But you were washed clean (purified by a complete atonement for sin and made free from the guilt of sin), and you were consecrated (set apart, hallowed), and you were justified [pronounced righteous, by trusting] in the name of the Lord Jesus Christ and in the [Holy] Spirit of our God (1 Corinthians 6:11).

The Bible is very clear that Christ has already accomplished the work of making you righteous. Jesus came to give us a new heart through the Holy Spirit because the old one was incurable. As a new-creation believer, you spiritually have a new heart.

*Then will I sprinkle clean water upon you, and you shall be clean from all your uncleanness; and from all your idols will I cleanse you. **A new heart will I give you and a new spirit will I put within you**, and I will take away the stony heart out of your flesh and give you a heart of flesh. And I will put my Spirit within you and cause you to walk in My statutes, and you shall heed My ordinances and do them* (Ezekiel 36:25-27).

*And **I will give them one heart** [a new heart] and I will put a new spirit within them; and I will take the stony [unnaturally hardened] heart out of their flesh, and will give them a heart of flesh [sensitive and responsive to the touch of their God], that they may walk in My statutes and keep My ordinances, and do them. And they shall be My people, and I will be their God* (Ezekiel 11:19-20).

*For this is the covenant that I will make with the house of Israel after those days, says the Lord: I will imprint My laws upon their minds, even upon their innermost thoughts and understanding, and **engrave them upon their hearts**; and I will be their God, and they shall be My people* (Hebrews 8:10).

You may say, "Come on, Jeff, do you honestly believe that I have a new heart and that I'm righteous? What about in Isaiah where it says that God's ways are not my ways and God's thoughts are not my thoughts?

For My thoughts are not your thoughts, neither are your ways My ways, says the Lord (Isaiah 55:8).

That verse is true. But again, we have been made new creations. God has not only given us a new heart and a new mind, but He has given us the very mind of Christ. With the mind of Christ, it is no longer true to say of us that our thoughts are not His thoughts and His ways are not our ways, even if you don't feel like it.

We are a *kainos*, a new being with a new nature; each of us is a new person altogether. The old, *arkhayos*, has passed away, has become extinct, has been executed—and behold you are brand-new!

We Reign as Royalty in Life

*because of one man's trespass (Adams lapse, offense) death reigned through that one, much more surely will those who receive [God's] overflowing grace (unmerited favor) and the free gift of righteousness [putting them into right standing with Himself] **reign as kings** in life through the one Man Jesus Christ (the Messiah, the Anointed One* (Romans 5:17).

Paul says we *"reign as kings in life through the one Man Jesus Christ."*

The problem is, we have too much of the world's influence on us and cannot see ourselves as supernatural sons and daughters of the King. Pastor Bill Johnson says, "If you want to kill giants, hang around giant killers." The influence will rub off. That's what happened with David and his mighty men.

For our sake He made Christ [virtually] to be sin Who knew no sin, so that in and through Him we might become [endued with, viewed as being in, and examples of] the righteousness of God [what we ought to be, approved and acceptable and in right relationship with Him, by His goodness] (2 Corinthians 5:21).

We have God's DNA

We have God's DNA. He exchanged His life for ours. He became sin so we could become righteous; and because of the exchange, we reign victorious as reigning royalty in life. As mentioned previously, it is abnormal for a Christian not to have an appetite for the impossible. It is written into our spiritual DNA to hunger for impossibilities and to see them bow at the name of Jesus.

We are God's very own family. When we are born of the Spirit we receive God's DNA, or as I call it, "Divine Nature Applied." It is His genetic code in us that cannot be changed or altered. This is a universal or creation law principal that applies to all created things.

Question: Can I birth a child who has a different genetic code from me?

Of course not! We can only reproduce according to the DNA we were born with, preprogrammed by God within. In my book *Glory Rising*, I call this "The Creation Law of Reproduction," which simply means that all things reproduce after their own kind.

Then God said, "Let the earth sprout vegetation, plants yielding seed, and fruit trees on the earth bearing fruit after their kind with seed in them"; and it was so. The earth brought forth vegetation, plants yielding seed after their kind; and God saw that it was good (Genesis 1:11-12 NASB).

Birds are birds; they bring forth birds after their own kind. Fish are fish; they bring forth fish each after their own kind and likeness. Cattle bring forth cattle, dogs produce dogs, horses produce horses, humans produce humans, and divinity produces divinity. Get it?

No one who is born of God practices sin, because His seed abides in him; and he cannot sin, because he is born of God (1 John 3:9 NASB).

The Greek word for seed is *sperma*. We have the divine *sperma* of God in our spirit. God's entire DNA is inside us.

Peter wrote that we are partakers of God's divine nature. God has given us a new nature. Actually, He has given us His nature:

By means of these He has bestowed on us His precious and exceedingly great promises, so that through them you may escape [by flight] from the moral decay (rottenness and corruption) that is in the world because of covetousness (lust and greed), and become sharers (partakers) of the divine nature (2 Peter 1:4).

See what [an incredible] quality of love the Father has given (shown, bestowed on) us, that we should [be permitted to] be named and called and counted the children of God! And so we are! The reason that the world does not know (recognize, acknowledge) us is that it does not know (recognize, acknowledge) Him.

Beloved, we are [even here and] now God's children; it is not yet disclosed (made clear) what we shall be [hereafter], but we know that when He comes and is manifested, we shall as God's children] resemble and be like Him, for we shall see Him just as He [really] is (1 John 3:1-2).

So, we are partakers of the divine nature. We are God's very own family, His children who are made like Him.

As He Is in the World, so Are We

In the same way that Jesus was full of God, so are we:

But the person who is united to the Lord becomes one spirit with Him (1 Corinthians 6:17).

The apostle John taught that we are designed to live just like Jesus did, and that:

In this [union and communion with Him] love is brought to completion and attains perfection with us, that we may have confidence for the day of judgment [with assurance and boldness to face Him], because as He is, so are we in this world (1 John 4:17).

This is not the Jesus of the past, but the Jesus of the present—the Jesus of the *now*. These are the attributes that describe us, those who receive God's unlimited grace and the gift of righteousness through the One Man, Jesus Christ. As He is, so are we in the world. If it is true of Jesus, it should also be true of us. The Bible teaches that God gave you a new heart, mind, and spirit. We are one spirit with God and filled with His fullness. This being true, is should be easy for us to see our enthronement with Him.

The more we live as citizens of Heaven, the more Heaven's activities infect our lifestyles.

If we can come into agreement with this Kingdom reality and believe it, then our lives and lives of those around us will drastically change.

You are a citizen of Heaven. You are a partaker of the divine nature. As He is in the world, so are you.

Enthroned as a New Creation

The truth is that we are one spirit with God and have already been filled with all the fullness of God.

> *For in Him the whole **fullness** of Deity (the Godhead) continues to dwell in bodily form [giving complete expression of the divine nature]. And you are in Him, made **full** and having come to **fullness** of life [in Christ you too are filled with the Godhead—Father, Son and Holy Spirit—and reach **full** spiritual stature]. And He is the Head of all rule and authority [of every angelic principality and power]* (Colossians 2:9-10).

Question: What is fullness? The apostle Paul says it is when we *"reach unity in the faith and in the knowledge of the Son of God and become mature."*

> *until we all reach unity in the faith and in the knowledge of the Son of God and become mature, attaining to the whole measure of the **fullness** of Christ* (Ephesians 4:13 NIV).

We are the righteousness of God in Christ and have become partakers of the divine nature. The Holy Spirit is working within to take the things of Jesus and reveal them to us. His death brings us into forgiveness. When the Holy Spirit reveals our identification with Him, this brings us into the *new-creation class* of righteousness.

Ultimately, as we behold our enthronement with him, we are released to participate in His dominion. We begin to reign consistently in life over the devil, sin, and sickness through Christ Jesus. As we begin to believe the reality of being heirs with Christ, we realize His amazing love for us.

As our revelation grows, the resurrection life of Christ Jesus is released to bring us into His image, and we are then able to appreciate our process of being conformed to His image. Our Father has begun a good work in us and will continue to perfect it until the day of Christ.

> *And I am convinced and sure of this very thing, that He Who began a good work in you **will continue** until the day of Jesus Christ [right up to the time of His return], developing [that good work] and **perfecting and bringing it to full completion in you*** (Philippians 1:6).

Our enthronement with Christ causes us to see that old things really have passed away and that we have immediate and complete authority over the dominion of the enemy. We are new creations in God. The Holy Spirit has been given to us to accomplish the task of continually unveiling these riches to us. He delights to bring us into these blessings.

CHAPTER 5

WE ARE CHRIST
TO THE WORLD

There is a strong emphasis coming in this season that will quickly become the hallmark theme of all we are to become as believers. This Kingdom reality will be the cornerstone of truth that will anchor the church of Jesus Christ to its original mandate, propelling the church into a re-awakening of sonship marked with powerful displays of the miraculous. This awakening will bring forth the transformation of churches, cities, regions, and whole nations. This awakening is "Christ in us," the hope of glory!

—Jeff Jansen

We are Christ to the world. I don't mean that we just preach Christ to the world. I mean people should experience Christ when they meet us because it is Jesus who is being formed in us. As a matter of fact, it is no longer we who live but Christ who lives in us (see Gal. 2:20).

When people hear Christians preaching the Word without also *becoming* the Word, the Gospel gets reduced to a mere philosophy—principles to be argued and words that can be wrangled over. But when the Word becomes flesh and dwells among us, people find themselves pierced to the heart and convicted in the depths of their very souls. It is incumbent upon us as the people of God to preach Christ wherever we go and, only when necessary, use words!

Ingestion Versus Digestion

When Jesus said we must eat His flesh and drink His blood, He wasn't talking about cannibalism, He was referring to ingestion that leads to incarnation. Christ is the Word that became flesh. It is important that we *ingest* the Word of God in a way that causes us to *digest* His life until Christ is formed within us. Ingestion without digestion will lead to feeling full, but not being transformed. Digestion is more than just a taste test; it is the full meal of His presence that conforms us to His image. The old saying is true: "You are what you eat!"

Many people ingest the Bible but don't digest the living, active Word of God. Religion fills their souls but never satisfies their longing for real life. Digestion requires assimilation, not just consumption. Truth was never meant to just be recounted; it was intended to be experienced. When we exchange the communion meal for a dinner commentary or a cookbook, we deprive ourselves of the privilege of abundant life and relegate ourselves to a meager existence in the Kingdom.

Jesus never intended for us to be full of religion; He desires us to be filled with His Spirit. Christ is the ultimate "happy meal," and as we digest Him, we become one flesh with Him. That is why Jesus prayed:

*That they all may be one, [just] as You, Father, are in Me and I in You, **that they also may be one in Us**, so that the world may believe and be convinced that You have sent Me. I have given to them the glory and honor which You have given Me, that they may be one [even] as We are one: **I in them and You in Me, in order that they may become one and perfectly united**, that the world may know and [definitely] recognize that You sent Me and that You have loved them [even] as You have loved Me* (John 17:21-23).

Christ is not talking about His disciples getting along with each other here. He was describing the unity between the bride and the Bridegroom, where the intimacy of intercourse assimilates us into one flesh. When we come to the communion table and eat the flesh of our King, we become an inseparable unity that causes the world to experience His presence every time they encounter us. In other words, when they see us, they have seen the Father.

Christ in Us

As stated previously, we are Christ to the world. When people meet us they are meeting Jesus Christ. Through us His Word becomes flesh again as we reveal Jesus to the world around us. It's a beautiful mystery that we should be His Body on earth: Christ to the world.

...Christ within and among you, the Hope of [realizing the] glory (Colossians 1:27).

...it is no longer I who live, but Christ (the Messiah) lives in me... (Galatians 2:20).

As we ingest Christ, we are becoming like Him. Paul prayed for the Galatian church and wrote:

My little children, for whom I am again suffering birth pangs until Christ is completely and permanently formed (molded) within you (Galatians 4:19).

There is maturing taking place. We are being changed, morphed, transformed into mature sons and daughters of God who rightly represent Him in the earth. The world is looking for the real Jesus Christ. As we eat and drink from Him, we are being changed.

The Family Business

We can describe the plan of God as simple. It is to extend the rule of His unseen Kingdom, or spirit world, into the visible Kingdom, or physical world, through a family of legal heirs—sons and daughters who are connected to the throne. These offspring will act as God, on behalf of God, being His legal representatives and judiciaries on the planet, to carry out His orders and implement His will with full governmental authority given to them by their Father and older heavenly Brother, Jesus.

From the dawn of time, life has been about family, and will continue to be so until the end days. It is about the Father and His children. It's high time for us to be about the Father's business. After the resurrection, Jesus told Mary, who was the first to see Him:

"Go to My brethren and say to them, 'I am ascending to My Father and your Father, to My God and your God" (John 20:17 NKJV).

The word "brethren" can also be translated "brothers." We are the siblings of Jesus. His Father is our Father, His God is our God. Jesus is the firstborn among many children:

For God knew his people in advance, and he chose them to become like his Son, so that his Son would be the firstborn among many brothers and sisters (Romans 8:29 NLT).

The only begotten Son of the Father, Jesus, is the prototype for the brothers and sisters who find their way to a relationship with the Father, and who become joint heirs with Christ of the coming Kingdom. Jesus was not ashamed to call us brothers because we are family with Him.

And to as many as received Him, to them He gave the right to become children of God, even to those who believe in His name (John 1:12 NKJV).

He gave us the right, ability, and privilege to become children of God when we believe in His name.

We are in a place in history where we are starting to see the children of God's Kingdom come into maturity. The seeds of coming-of-age are visibly beginning to bring forth fruit that resembles the fruit of the original *Seed,* Jesus Christ. Through His offspring, God is manifesting and establishing His Kingdom and His will on planet Earth. He rules the seen world from the unseen world through us as He births His initiatives in the physical world.

The fruitful journey of Jesus was well-documented as He traveled to cities and villages, teaching in their synagogues, proclaiming the good news of the Kingdom of God. He cured *every* sickness, disease, and infirmity that He encountered (see Matt. 4:23; 9:35), further preparing the soil and sowing afresh the precious seed.

Everywhere He preached the Gospel, Jesus manifested His power with wild miracles, signs, and wonders. God expects His offspring, His family, His seed to do the same works—acting the same way Jesus did.

Because you are sons, God has sent forth the Spirit of His Son into your hearts, crying out, "Abba! Father!" Therefore you are no longer a slave but a son, and if a son, then an heir of God through Christ (Galatians 4:6-7 NKJV).

Adam's rebellion toward God ended in spiritual death resulting in him being cut off from the throne and access to unhindered supernatural ability. Adam was left to find his own way in this life, filtering the world around him through his five natural senses.

But now, that which was covered deep in the spirit of humankind has been uncovered by the sacrificial blood offering of our older Brother and Lord Jesus Christ and is now being discovered again in this age and time, and understood afresh by a family of sons and daughters of God all around the world. All things have been put in subjection under the feet of Christ. We are the Body of Christ—so all things have been put under our feet.

The Spirit of Heirship and Glory

Satan is a copier and a liar. When the Church rises in revelation and understanding of who we are and who Jesus is within us, the world will see the mature Body of Jesus Christ operate just as Jesus did 2,000 years ago in a single body, moving in miracles, healings, signs, and wonders. What He did then, He is doing now in a greater way through a fully mature, corporately anointed body of believers.

It's nothing less than the divine and holy seed—that divine sperm growing us into full maturity. As we enter into this revelation as a family of legal sons and daughters—nothing will be impossible for us. As we speak, our words will become substance in glory, and matter will be created. The elements must obey the voices of the family of God—God designed things this way.

All things belong to you, all things are yours, you can do all things because hidden treasures of wisdom, knowledge, and revelation *are in* Jesus Christ, and fully accessible to you.

Branded Children of God

When Adam and Eve were brought forth, God had a family. Think about what this really meant to God. He had a family on the earth.

We know that through the Fall, man gave up his position and in turn became the sons of the enemy and took upon his likeness and his image. But through the cross and the blood of Jesus, God remedied the situation. John tells us:

> *But to as many as did received and welcome Him, He gave the authority (power, privilege, right) to become the children of God, that is, to those who believe in (adhere to, trust in, and rely on) His name* (John 1:12).

John goes on to say:

> *Who owe their birth neither to bloods nor to the will of the flesh [that of physical impulse] nor to the will of man [that of a natural father], but to God. [They are born of God!]* (John 1:13).

When Paul wrote to the churches at Galatia and Ephesus, telling them that his intention for them was the perfecting and full equipping of the saints until they were mature, he was bearing all of the history and design of man in mind. Paul told the Galatians in chapter 4 verse 19 that he was actually suffering birth pangs until Christ was completely and permanently formed (molded) within them.

There is a maturing taking place—a coming to fullness of all the seeds of the Kingdom that have been sown in our hearts. The things we have known in a limited measure are being made fully known. This reawakening Body of Christ is coming forth in the full power of Heaven and will fill the whole earth with the knowledge of the glory of God.

This is the Church's finest hour. Before the second coming of Jesus Christ, the mature children of the Kingdom will shine like no other generation in human history. This shining forth will be nothing less than Christ in us, the hope of glory!

> *To whom God was pleased to make known how great for the Gentiles are the riches of the glory of this mystery, which is Christ within and among you, the Hope of [realizing the] glory* (Colossians 1:27).

The Human Spirit

We are not human beings having a spiritual experience, we are spiritual beings having a human experience.

—*Jeff Jansen*

Your spirit is the real you. You are a spirit who has a soul who lives in a body on the earth. God is breaking our outer self so that we can live from our spirit and not our soul. The reality for many Spirit-filled believers is that their spirits are encased within the soul, unable to emerge, trapped by the physical body and beat down by appetites of the flesh. But God is cracking the outer core so the Holy Spirit will beam out from our spirits.

God put His own genetic code in your spirit. His seed abides in you—encased in your spirit. You are born not of a corruptible seed but an incorruptible seed by the Word of God that lives and abides inside you. Every Spirit-filled believer is born of incorruptible seed:

No one who is born of God practices sin, because His seed abides in him; and he cannot sin, because he is born of God (1 John 3:9 NASB).

In the natural, all of the father's DNA is in the seed—and it says a lot about how his child will turn out: hair color, eye color, even personality type. Our genetic makeup is programmed in the father's seed.

You were *born again* of the seed of God. All of God's DNA is resident within you. The spiritual genetic code of God was placed in you, and in it are all of the characteristics of the Lord. Now if all of that seed in you reaches maturity, who do you think you will be like? Jesus! That seed is inside you. You do not have to struggle to get those characteristics: they are all within you, already there.

CHAPTER 6

GLORIOUS ESCHATOLOGY—AN OPTIMISTIC WORLDVIEW

For too long now the church has been riddled with fear because of bad theology and misinterpretation of Scripture as it relates to end-time theology. History alone backs up what took place in AD 70 with the destruction of the temple and the end of animal sacrifice. This was the undisputed historical view of all our forefathers and theologians until the dawn of the 20th century. It's time for a clear picture to emerge within the church that biblically and historically energizes her with a glorious eschatology. We are to think long range and bring revival to the nations that will transform the earth.

—Jeff Jansen

In order for us to know what our future holds and how it relates to our enthronement with Christ, it is absolutely crucial that we understand where we are in human history and how it relates to end-time theology or what many refer to as the "End of the Age." If we are to have hope for the future in the Kingdom of God, we must have a better understanding for God's biblical timeline as it relates to the second coming of Jesus Christ.

My aim in this chapter is to point to the bright future of the church as ambassadors of the Kingdom of God and to establish a proper biblical and historical grid so we can move with full assurance into the nations of the earth with the Gospel of Good News.

The following is a statement of core values, written by Kris Vallotton, that I personally hold to be accurate and true. I would ask that you consider them as they are, and what most Bible historians and theologians for the past two millennia believe to be, an accurate biblical and historical perspective.

1. I will not embrace an end-time worldview that re-empowers a disempowered devil.
2. I will not accept an eschatology that takes away my children's future and creates mindsets that undermine the mentality of leaving them with a legacy.
3. I will not tolerate any theology that negates the clear command of Jesus to make disciples of all nations and the Lord's Prayer that earth would be like Heaven.
4. I will not accept any interpretation of Scripture that destroys hope for revival in the nations and undermines our command to restore ruined cities.
5. I will not embrace an eschatology that changes the nature of a good God.
6. I refuse to embrace any mindset that celebrates bad news as a sign of the end-times and a necessary requirement for the return of Jesus Christ.

7. I am opposed to any doctrinal position that pushes the promises of God into a time zone that can't be obtained in my generation and therefore takes away any responsibility I have to believe God for them in my lifetime.

8. I do not believe that the last days are a time of judgment, nor do I believe God gave the church the right to call for wrath for sinful cities. There is a day of judgment in which GOD will judge man, not us.[1]

In his book *Raptureless,* Jonathan Welton states:

Every part of the Gospel is simple, including the teaching regarding the end-times. If something is too complex for the average person to grasp, then it is being taught wrongly. Our view of the future should not cause fear. No part of the Gospel (which literally means "good news") ever causes fear. Our understanding of the end-times determines how we live our lives and whether we plan long-term, build a legacy, prepare our children for a lifetime of service to the Lord, and so forth. A correct view of the end-times will set us free from fear. It will cause us to have a renewed passion for Jesus rather than an obsession with the antichrist.

Much of the following information in this chapter comes from my good friend Jonathan Welton. Jonathan is the founding professor of Welton Academy and holds a Doctorate in Theology. I've included the following excerpts in this chapter from his astounding books *Raptureless* and *The Art of Revelation,* which I recommend for further study. I, along with many others, find his work to be biblically and historically accurate. My aim here is to encourage you of your position and mandate in the Kingdom of God—not go into graphic detail about end-time theology.

Jesus came to preach and demonstrate the power of the Kingdom, and it has been growing on the earth for the past 2,000 years. It will continue to grow until the mountain of the Lord becomes the largest of all the mountains on the earth as Daniel 2:44 and Isaiah 2:2 state. We, as the Church of Jesus Christ, are in the greatest place in human history, and it is only going to get better.

Again, the following is just a brief overview of what our forefathers in the faith and historical theologians believed, including Charles Spurgeon, John Wesley, John Calvin, and others. We need to have an optimistic worldview and correct understanding of the times in order to bring the power of the Gospel of the Kingdom into the nations of the earth. Our enthronement with Christ demands that we have a proper understanding so we can move with confidence into a glorious future with the Lord Jesus Christ.

Jesus' Prophecy in Matthew 24

The main passage used to paint this picture comes from the prophecy of Jesus in Matthew 24. Most scholars agree that the book of Revelation is a parallel to the words of Jesus in Matthew 24, but because I am writing a simple introduction, and for of lack of space, I will not be addressing Revelation in this book. Matthew 24 is the passage that predicts earthquakes, famines, plagues, false teachers, and Jesus' coming on the clouds.

However, as I studied Matthew 24, I discovered that, throughout Church history, most Christians believed that the whole of Matthew chapter 27, when Jesus spoke about the temple being destroyed, occurred at the destruction of Jerusalem in AD 70 and was not something He put way off into the future.

Truly I tell you, this generation (the whole multitude of people living at the same time, in a definite, given period) will not pass away till all these things taken together take place (Matthew 24:34).

In fact, many of the well-known church leaders have taught this. For example:

All this occurred in this manner in the second year of the reign of Vespasian [A.D. 70], according to the predictions of our Lord and Saviour Jesus Christ. —Eusebius

Thousands and thousands of men of every age who together with women and children perished by the sword, by starvation, and by countless other forms of death...all this anyone who wishes can gather in precise detail from the pages of Josephus's history. I must draw particular attention to his statement that the people who flocked together from all Judaea at the time of the Passover Feast and—to use his own words—were shut up in Jerusalem as if in a prison, totaled nearly three million. —Eusebius

This was most punctually fulfilled: for after the temple was burned, Titus the Roman general, ordered the very foundations of it to be dug up; after which the ground on which it stood was ploughed by Turnus Rufus...this generation of men living shall not pass till all these things be done— The expression implies that a great part of that generation would be passed away, but not the whole. Just so it was; for the city and temple were destroyed thirty-nine or forty years after. —John Wesley

You will preach everywhere.... Then he added, "This gospel of the kingdom will be preached throughout the whole

world, as a testimony to all nations; and the end will come."
The sign of this final end time will be the downfall of Jerusalem. —John Chrysostom

There was a sufficient interval for the full proclamation
of the Gospel by the apostles and evangelists of the early
Christian Church, and for the gathering of those who
recognized the crucified Christ as the true Messiah. Then
came the awful end, which the Saviour foresaw and fore-
told, and the prospect of which wrung from His lips and
heart the sorrowful lament that followed his prophecy of
the doom awaiting his guilty capital.

The destruction of Jerusalem was more terrible than anything that the world has ever witnessed, either before or
since. Even Titus seemed to see in his cruel work the hand
of an avenging God. Truly, the blood of the martyrs slain in
Jerusalem was amply avenged when the whole city became
a veritable Aceldama, or field of blood. —Charles Spurgeon

Christ informs them, that before a single generation shall
have been completed, they will learn by experience the
truth of what he has said. For within fifty years the city
was destroyed and the temple was razed, the whole country
was reduced to a hideous desert. —John Calvin

The Historical Development

The Reformation of the 1500s changed a lot of things, but unwit-
tingly it eventually affected the end-time beliefs of much of the
Church. In the early 1500s, Martin Luther railed against the
Roman Catholic Church and, in his passion, he called her the

Whore of Babylon and the Beast. To counter this, in 1585 a Jesuit priest by the name of Francisco Ribera published a 500-page work that placed Daniel 9:24-27, Matthew 24, and Revelation 4–19 in the distant future. This was the first thought of its kind, and it is the foundation of many modern end-time views. The significance of this new interpretation is that rather than seeing these passages as fulfilled, Ribera said they were still to come.

Historically speaking, Ribera's new view did not gain momentum. In fact, his writing was lost until 1826 when Samuel Maitland, librarian to the Archbishop of Canterbury, discovered Ribera's forgotten manuscript and published it for the sake of public interest and curiosity.

When the book resurfaced, a small group of ultra-conservatives, led by John Darby, began to take Ribera's book seriously and came under the influence of this thinking. John Darby and his contemporary, Edward Irving, became extremely vocal about their new theology of the end-times and attracted many followers. Their most important follower was C. I. Scofield, who later published these concepts in his famed Scofield Reference Bible.

The Scofield Bible was the most popular of its time because it was one of the earliest Bibles to contain a full commentary. It quickly became a standard for seminary students of the time. This continued unchallenged until the 1948 Latter Rain movement, which disagreed with the Scofield Reference Bible's claims that the spiritual gifts had ceased. The Pentecostals pushed back against these portions of the commentary but still swallowed Ribera's end-time teachings without refute.

Then in 1961, Finis Dake published the Dake's Annotated Reference Bible, which continued to promote the same Darbyism as the Scofield Bible, and the Ryrie and MacArthur Study Bibles have continued this tradition of Darbyism.

Thus we see that Martin Luther's attack against the Roman Catholic Church caused one priest to react by writing a new doctrine. This began the belief that certain prophecies have not yet been fulfilled.

The Late Great Planet Earth Shake Down

In 1970, Hal Lindsey wrote *The Late, Great Planet Earth*. Approximately 35 million copies were sold, which deeply affected a generation of pastors and leaders growing up in the Jesus People Movement of the early 1970s. The lasting fruit of this book has created a generation who believe more in Lindsey's mythology than understanding what the Bible and history actually teach.

Later, Hal Lindsey released another book titled *The 1980s: Countdown to Armageddon*, implying that the battle of Armageddon would happen soon. He even went so far as to say, "The decade of the 1980s could very well be the last decade of history as we know it," and suggested that the United States would be destroyed by a surprise Soviet attack. Not surprisingly, because of Lindsey's adamant insistence that the 1980s would usher in the Great Tribulation, the book was quietly taken out of print in the early 1990s.

Lindsey, however, did not give up. In the early 1990s, he published *Planet Earth—2000 A.D.*, which warns Christians that they should not plan on living on earth by the year 2000.

Throughout his several books, Lindsey assumed that the Cold War would continue until the end and, in fact, would play a significant part in the unfolding of end-time events. He even named Russia as the famous Gog of Revelation 20:8. Likewise, Lindsey believed the hippie culture of the 1960s and '70s would become the dominant culture in the United States, ultimately leading to the immorality and false religion "prophesied" to arise in the end times by various Bible passages.

Clearly, none of these prophecies came to pass and many have been proven wrong due to the dates ascribed to them, yet Lindsey is still lauded by many Christians as a great modern-day prophet.

Then in 1995, the first of the mega-bestselling book series, *Left Behind*, was released. Due to the paranoia and fear regarding Y2K (the transition from the year 1999 to 2000), Christians were primed for rapture fever. When all was said and done, Y2K turned out to be nothing more than hype, and 60 million copies of *Left Behind* had been sold (as well as three, in my opinion, terrible feature length films that were similar in nature and theology to the *Thief in the Night* movie series of the 1970s).

Now we are in the new millennium, and it is high time that we begin to deeply question the modern end-time views. If a teacher has been proclaiming that the end of the world is coming soon for over forty years, we should stop paying attention. If a teacher has proclaimed over forty different people to be the antichrist, we should ignore him. The fact that these teachers wear suits and appear on television doesn't make them any less wrong than the crazy guy on the street corner wearing a sandwich board sign that reads, "The end is near!" If a teacher, who had also been a paranoid Y2K alarmist, tried to sell you on the next end-of-the-world warning, I'm fairly certain you wouldn't listen too closely about his new futuristic proclamations.

The Advancing Kingdom of God

That being said, there are those who believe that the Kingdom of God will arrive all at once in the future. They say that God's Kingdom will instantly triumph over all the powers of the devil when it finally appears. This idea comes from thinking that we are currently in the "Church Age" and are awaiting the arrival of the "Kingdom Age." It's very clear that when Jesus arrived in human history, He came preaching the Gospel of the Kingdom, saying:

> *But if I drive out demons by the finger of God, then the kingdom of God has come upon you* (Luke 11:20).

It is very clear that the Kingdom of God arrived with Jesus in the year He was born. Take a good look at the nature of this gradually advancing and ever-increasing Kingdom.

The Ever-Increasing Kingdom of God

Jesus came to set up His Kingdom and said that it would continually grow. He used these two analogies to describe this aspect of the Kingdom:

> *The Kingdom of Heaven is like a mustard seed planted in a field. It is the smallest of all seeds, but it becomes the largest of garden plants; it grows into a tree, and birds come and make nests in its branches* (Matthew 13:31-32 NLT).

> *The Kingdom of Heaven is like the yeast a woman used in making bread. Even though she put only a little yeast in three measures of flour, it permeated every part of the dough* (Matthew 13:33 NASB).

As Daniel says:

> *In the time of those kings, the God of heaven will set up a kingdom that will never be destroyed, nor will it be left to another*

people. It will crush all those kingdoms and bring them to an end, but it will itself endure forever (Daniel 2:44 NASB).

This verse is reminiscent of Isaiah 9 that says:

Of the increase of His government and peace there will be no end (Isaiah 9:7 NKJV).

The nature of the Kingdom of God is ever progressing—always expanding, never retreating or backing off, and continually growing. Take, for example, the following five progressive statements from Scripture. The Word says that we move from:

1. Brighter to Brighter

The path of the righteous is like the morning sun, shining ever brighter till the full light of day (Proverbs 4:18 NIV).

2. Grace to Grace

And of His fullness we have all received, and grace for grace (John 1:16 NKJV).

3. Strength to Strength

They go from strength to strength (Psalm 84:7 NKJV).

4. Faith to Faith

For in it the righteousness of God is revealed from faith to faith; as it is written, "The just shall live by faith" (Romans 1:17 NKJV).

5. Glory to Glory

But we all, with unveiled face, beholding as in a mirror the glory of the Lord, are being transformed into the same image from glory to glory, just as by the Spirit of the Lord (2 Corinthians 3:18 NKJV).

According to these verses, we can accurately say that the Church is currently walking in the greatest brightness, grace, strength, faith, and glory that it ever has. This is very hard for some to accept, but it is true. Jesus set in motion a Kingdom that is still progressing and being established more and more each day. *"Of the increase of His government and peace there shall be no end"* (Isaiah 9:7 NKJV). It will continue to progress until it has fulfilled the following verses:

...For the earth will be filled with the knowledge of the Lord as the waters cover the sea (Isaiah 11:9 NKJV).

For the earth will be filled with the knowledge of the glory of the Lord, as the waters cover the sea (Habakkuk 2:14 NKJV).

But truly, as I live, all the earth shall be filled with the glory of the Lord (Numbers 14:21 NKJV).

The Advancing Kingdom

It is important to understand that Jesus set up His Kingdom upon His first visit. Many have been taught that Jesus set up the "Church Age" and that we are not currently living in the "Kingdom Age." They believe the Church Age will continue until Jesus' return, at which point He will initiate the Kingdom Age. Scripture does not support this point of view in any way. Jesus clearly brought His Kingdom with Him.

From that time on Jesus began to preach, "Repent, for the kingdom of heaven has come near" (Matthew 4:17 NIV).

Jesus also sent His disciples to preach the Gospel of the Kingdom, and not the Gospel of the Church Age.

As you go, proclaim this message: "The kingdom of heaven has come near." Heal the sick, raise the dead, cleanse those who have leprosy, drive out demons. Freely you have received; freely give (Matthew 10:7-8 NIV).

The whole concept of a Church Age cannot be found in Scripture. The Kingdom arrived in the first century when "the rock cut without hands"—Jesus—crashed into the Roman Empire, and it has been growing ever since.

Many who don't understand that Jesus and His Kingdom (as established during the first century) are "the rock cut without hands" from Nebuchadnezzar's dream, also believe the Roman Empire has to be rebuilt so that Jesus can crash into it *in the future* in order to set up His Kingdom. Fortunately, this has already been accomplished. Jesus completely fulfilled Daniel 2 in the first century, and there is no reason to revive the Roman Empire so that Jesus can fulfill this prophecy twice.

What of the Remnant?

We have established that the Kingdom Jesus set up is progressing and advancing all the time. The next question that arises is about remnant theology. In the Old Testament, we observe a pattern of the "faithful remnant." In other words, often only a minority or a small group of people were actually faithful to God. For example, out of all the people on the face of the earth, only eight survived the flood on Noah's ark (see Gen. 8). Out of all of Gideon's men, only 300 fought in the battle (see Judg. 7). Out of all the inhabitants of Sodom and Gomorrah, only Lot and his daughters survived (see Gen. 19). This is a common pattern in the Old Testament.

Many people carry the idea of the remnant over from the Old Testament into the New Testament, yet this is not the nature of the Kingdom that Jesus established. Rather, the remnant concept is reversed in the Kingdom of God. Under Jesus, out of twelve disciples, He only lost one, Judas (see John 17:12). The Kingdom starts as a seed and grows to the biggest tree.

> *He told them another parable: "The kingdom of heaven is like a mustard seed, which a man took and planted in his field. Though it is the smallest of all seeds, yet when it grows, it is the largest of garden plants and becomes a tree, so that the birds come and perch in its branches"* (Matthew 13:31-32 NIV).

It starts as a little leaven and works through the whole loaf. It starts as a stone cut without hands and grows into a mountain that fills the whole earth.

> *Then the iron, the clay, the bronze, the silver and the gold were all broken to pieces and became like chaff on a threshing floor in the summer. The wind swept them away without leaving a trace. But the rock that struck the statue became a huge mountain and filled the whole earth* (Daniel 2:35 NIV).

> *In the last days the mountain of the Lord's temple will be established as the highest of the mountains; it will be exalted above*

the hills, and all nations will stream to it. Many peoples will come and say, "Come, let us go up to the mountain of the Lord, to the temple of the God of Jacob. He will teach us his ways, so that we may walk in his paths…" (Isaiah 2:2-3 NIV).

The New Testament holds no room for remnant thinking. This defeatist mindset, which sees only a portion of the whole Church as good, needs to be set aside along with animal sacrifice and certain other Old Testament realities that are no longer valid.

Endnote

1. Vallotton, Kris. "My 8 Eschatological Core Values." Kris Vallotton, 22 Dec. 2017, krisvallotton.com/my-8-eschatological-core-values/.

CHAPTER 7

GLORIOUS ESCHATOLOGY— HISTORICAL PERSPECTIVE

M any Christians have a hard time viewing the future opti-
mistically because they lack perspective regarding the
past. When they look back, they think that they are seeing "the
good ole' days." However, with a better grasp on history, we will
see that God's Kingdom has, in fact, been steadily progressing forward. To see this improvement, we must lift ourselves to a higher
perspective from which we can look over the course of history. We
know what life is like today; compare it to the conditions of society
in the past.

The Early 1800s

First, look at what life was like in the United States 200 years ago,
in the early 1800s. At that time, the population was slightly over
5 million, but 20 percent of those people were slaves (that's more
than 1 million slaves). Abortion was legal during most of the 19th
century, and according to the records, one fifth of all pregnancies

were aborted (Michigan had the highest rate at 34 percent). Also, in many states, the age of sexual consent was as low as nine or ten years old, and prostitution was commonplace. New York City estimated having a ratio of one prostitute to every 64 men and Savannah, Georgia, estimated a ratio of 1 to 39.

This was also the time of the pioneers and covered wagon trains heading westward. Thousands relocated to the "Wild West," looking for gold and a fresh start. When gold was discovered in 1849, the gold rushes created some of the most despicable and dangerous communities. In fact, throughout the West, murder was so common that most people carried a gun for protection. Even in safer frontier communities, no organized churches were formed until years after settlements had been established. At the same time, tens of thousands of American Indians were murdered or forced from their lands, and thousands of Chinese people were imported as slaves.

During that time period, women had virtually no rights. Not only were women not allowed to vote, but their husbands were legally allowed to beat them as long as they avoided maiming or killing them. Also, alcoholism occurred at a much higher rate than it does today.

Although some godly people were laying the foundations for the U.S. government and other good things were happening, from these simple statistics we can plainly see that morally, ethically, and spiritually, the climate of the United States was far worse than it is today.

The Time of Jesus' Childhood

Looking even farther back in time, examine the climate of the whole world approximately 2,000 years ago—the time when

Jesus was a child. The Roman Empire ruled the world, with its primary cultural centers located in Europe, the Middle East, and Northern Africa. Throughout the empire, slavery was commonplace—to the point that in Italy, the hub of the empire, about 40 percent of the population were slaves. Homosexuality was also the norm, especially between masters and slaves. Many babies were killed after birth because they were deformed or sickly, or even simply female.

Obviously at that time, since Jesus was still a child, the Gospel had not yet arrived on the scene. The Jews had a revelation of God, yet they lived in disobedience and it had been 400 years since a prophet had spoken on God's behalf. Rather, most people worshipped a multitude of cruel and capricious gods, including Jupiter, Juno, and Neptune. Temple prostitution and ritual child sacrifice were regular parts of this religious system.

This was also the era of the gladiators; and in the Roman arenas, people were regularly tortured to death or mauled by wild animals. Later, under Nero, this fate befell many of the early Christians. It is hard for us to understand, but the philosophers that Western society so praises—Plato, Aristotle, and Socrates—saw nothing wrong with these practices. Ernest Hampden Cook, in his book *The Christ Has Come*, writes:

> The fact is that bad as the world still is, yet morally it is vastly better than it was when Jesus was born in Bethlehem of Judea.... Few people in these days have an adequate conception of the misery and degradation, which were then the common lot of almost all mankind, owing the monstrous wickedness of the times, to continual wars, to the cruelties of political despotism, and of everywhere-prevailing slavery.

Outside of the Roman Empire, things were no better. In Africa, Asia, and Australia, people worshipped nature, demons, and their deceased ancestors.

In North America, the Native Americans had many forms of worship; and in South America, tens of thousands of people were regularly sacrificed to a bloodthirsty pagan god. Yet throughout the whole world, no one knew the Messiah.

Truly, as we can see from this brief overview, the world was lost in darkness beyond what most of us can even imagine. This is what the apostle Paul meant when he wrote:

> *Formerly you, the Gentiles...were at that time separated from Christ...having no hope and without God in the world* (Ephesians 2:11-12).

Christianity Today

By comparison, examine the world today. The Gospel is reaching even the remotest places in the world, and Christianity is experiencing phenomenal growth globally. In fact, worldwide, more than 200,000 people are being born again daily. In China, it's 20,000 a day, and in South America, 35,000 a day. That adds up to more than 1 million people who are becoming Christians every week. The tiny seed that came to the earth in that small nation of Israel has grown to permeate the earth. Christianity is, in fact, the largest and most influential force of humanity in the world today.

Certainly, I am not saying our world is perfect or that global peace and utopia are just around the corner. Until Jesus' return, the struggle between light and dark will continue. Difficult times of war, famine, disease, and poverty may yet happen in the future, and during such times, people are often capable of the most inhumane acts. I am not denying the reality that life is sometimes tragic and excruciatingly painful.

But I also want to highlight the definite reality that, though it is not anywhere near perfect living here on earth, it is consistently becoming morally, ethically, and spiritually better. We must be watchful and hard at work, for we still have much to accomplish before Christ's return, but we must do this with the understanding that we are gaining ground, not losing it. The increase of God's government and peace is truly without end.

James Rutz, author of *Megashift*, states that the growing core of Christianity crosses theological lines and includes 707 million born-again people, a number that is increasing by 8 percent each year (this number excludes those groups that have essentially stopped growing because they are "so liberal in theology, so isolated in structure, or so rooted in…tradition"). This growing core of Christianity is comprised primarily of Charismatics, Pentecostals, and Evangelicals—their main characteristic being that they are part of "expanding, connected, and easily countable networks."

Though straight projections never work, it is interesting to note, as Rutz does, that the current growth rate would create a world composed entirely of what he calls "Apostolic Christians" by 2032. In fact, with tongue-in-cheek, Rutz tells us that, according to statistics, by the fall of 2032, there will be more Christians than people on the earth.

The new realities Rutz is pointing at are clear: "The future of your world is being written at this very hour." For example, Rutz points out:

- Until 1960, Western evangelicals outnumbered non-Western (Latino, Black, and Asian) evangelicals two to one.
- In 2000, non-Western evangelicals had surpassed Westerners four to one.

- Latin America, traditionally a Catholic region, now has more evangelicals attending church on a Sunday morning than Catholics.
- In India, "as soon as we produce some church models that are culturally acceptable to Hindus," we may see between 70 and 100 million secret Indian Christians come forth.
- More missionaries are now sent from non-Western nations than from Western nations.

These facts about the new realities of Christianity are somewhat mind boggling. As Rutz says, "God writes history, but human eyes have trouble reading his handwriting. It's not that he writes too small, but too big."

When the Spirit was first poured out on the early church, 3,000 people were saved in one day. That was amazing because, back then, it was a huge number. Today however, approximately 3,000 people get saved, somewhere in the world, every 25 minutes. The math is almost overwhelming.

According to Rutz, these numbers often happen through large events, such as the crusade that Reinhard Bonnke held in Lagos, Nigeria, in November 2000. During those six days and nights, almost 6 million people attended, and 3.4 million registered decisions to follow Christ, over 1 million of them being on the final night. One important element of such events is the widespread healing of all kinds of physical deformities, diseases, and illnesses through the power of the Holy Spirit. At Bonnke's Nigeria event, more than 1,000 physicians were present to examine people and confirm healings. Bonnke also had 30,000 ushers and spent the six months prior training 200,000 counselors to assist the many converts.

Such massive influxes of new believers are not isolated events, but are increasingly becoming common occurrences. Some have even estimated the advent of one billion new converts within ten years. "From our vantage point in North America and Europe, where church membership is going nowhere, this sounds like a cooked-up fantasy," Rutz says. "But it is true. This is the biggest megashift in history. Can you think of any time when over a billion people eagerly changed their lives and loyalties in one generation?"

Looking at the statistics, we can clearly see that, if growth continues at this rate, whole nations will experience transformation on all levels. In fact, as Rutz predicts, "We are in the early stages of a total transformation of our planet."

The point of these statistics is clear. The "good ole' days" were not as good as many of us assumed they were. When we remove our romanticized lenses in order to see what really was, as well as what is really happening *now,* we can clearly see that God's Kingdom is markedly advancing.

The Kingdom and the Church

Although a lot of the passages that are taught as future are actually past, I do also believe there are many passages of Scripture that remain to be fulfilled. These passages mainly fall into two categories: The Kingdom of God and the Church.

I define the Kingdom of God as His rulership, or in other words, the King's domain (Kingdom). Therefore, the Kingdom is God's sphere of rulership. As mentioned earlier, Jesus taught that the Kingdom of God was growing and expanding (see Matt. 13:31-33; Is. 9:7), that God's rulership is ever increasing from glory to glory. The Kingdom primarily grows through God's representatives on earth—His Church. Jesus placed the keys of the Kingdom into the hands of Peter as the representative of the Church.

And I tell you that you are Peter, and on this rock I will build my church, and the gates of Hades will not overcome it. I will give you the keys of the kingdom of heaven; whatever you bind on earth will be bound in heaven, and whatever you loose on earth will be loosed in heaven (Matthew 16:18-19 NIV).

Therefore, the Church on earth is working as God's representatives to expand and grow the Kingdom and His government without end. The ultimate end will be *"on earth as it is in Heaven"* (see Matt. 6:10). With this understanding, examine a few passages about the Kingdom that I believe are yet to be fulfilled, and then others regarding the Church that also have yet to pass.

The Kingdom

In Luke 19, Jesus told a parable:

He said therefore, A certain nobleman went into a far country to receive for himself a kingdom, and to return. And he called his ten servants, and delivered them ten pounds, and said unto them, Occupy till I come (Luke 19:12-13 KJV).

Jesus went to a far country (Heaven) to receive for Himself a Kingdom, and He will someday return. When Jesus left, He put stewardship into the hands of His servants (the Church). To *occupy* is to aggressively expand. The servants took the finances they were given and multiplied them. We are called to occupy the Kingdom, to advance it on earth, to be part of its growth from glory to glory. *We are to occupy until He comes, not be preoccupied with His coming.* As the prophet Isaiah wrote:

Of the increase of his government and peace there shall be no end, upon the throne of David, and upon his kingdom, to order it, and to establish it with judgment and with justice from henceforth even forever. The zeal of the Lord of hosts will perform this (Isaiah 9:7 KJV).

The Kingdom of God started growing at Jesus' first coming and will continue to grow until it culminates in His final return. As Jesus put it in another parable:

Another parable put he forth unto them, saying, The kingdom of heaven is like to a grain of mustard seed, which a man took, and sowed in his field: Which indeed is the least of all seeds: but when it is grown, it is the greatest among herbs, and becomes a tree, so that the birds of the air come and lodge in the branches thereof. Another parable spoke he unto them; The kingdom of heaven is like unto leaven, which a woman took, and hid in three measures of meal, till the whole was leavened (Matthew 13:31-33 KJV).

The Kingdom will continue to grow until His glory and knowledge fill the whole earth.

For the earth will be filled with the knowledge of the Lord as the waters cover the sea (Isaiah 11:9).

For the earth will be filled with the knowledge of the glory of the Lord, as the waters cover the sea (Habakkuk 2:14).

Currently, Jesus is sitting on the throne, waiting until all His enemies are made into His footstool.

When the Lord Jesus had finished talking with them, he was taken up into heaven and sat down in the place of honor at God's right hand (Mark 16:19 NLT).

But our High Priest offered himself to God as a single sacrifice for sins, good for all time. Then he sat down in the place of honor at God's right hand. There he waits until his enemies are humbled and made a footstool under his feet (Hebrews 10:12-13 NLT).

After that comes the end (the completion), when He delivers over the kingdom to God the Father after rendering inoperative and abolishing every [other] rule and every authority and power. For [Christ] must be King and reign until He has put all [His] enemies under His feet. The last enemy to be subdued and abolished is death (1 Corinthians 15:24-26).

Jesus has been sitting at the right hand of God for nearly 2,000 years, waiting; while His Church builds Him a divine footstool of sorts. The assignment of the Church for the last two millennia has been to crush satan under our feet.

The God of peace will soon crush Satan under your feet... (Romans 16:20).

As delegated authorities, by crushing satan under our feet, we are also placing him under Jesus' feet. Ultimately, satan is placed under our feet as members of Christ's Body. We are part of a progressive destruction of the demonic kingdom that will continue until death, the final enemy, is destroyed.

The ultimate goal is that His Kingdom will come in its full force and His *"will be done on earth as it is in heaven"* (Matt. 6:10). The signs of the times that Jesus listed in Matthew 24 were only in reference to AD 70. Therefore, the true signs that we look for in these days are the evidence of the growth of His Kingdom on planet Earth.

The Church

1. The Church in Unity

Jesus' famous prayer for unity in the Church is recorded in John 17.

> *That they may all be one; even as You, Father, are in Me and I in You, that they also may be in Us, so that the world may believe that You sent Me. The glory which You have given Me I have given to them, that they may be one, just as We are one; I in them and You in Me, that they may be perfected in unity, so that the world may know that You sent Me, and loved them, even as You have loved Me* (John 17:21-23 NASB).

The apostle Paul echoed Jesus' call for unity in his description of the fivefold ministry.

> *And He gave some as apostles, and some as prophets, and some as evangelists, and some as pastors and teachers, for the equipping of the saints for the work of service, to the building up of the body of Christ; until we all attain to the unity of the faith, and of the knowledge of the Son of God, to a mature man, to the measure of the stature which belongs to the fullness of Christ* (Ephesians 4:11-13 NASB).

According to David B. Barrett's *World Christian Encyclopedia*, there are 33,830 Christian denominations in the world today. I would say that we have not yet reached "unity in the faith."

One of the largest hindrances to arriving at the "unity of the faith" is an expectancy of the last days apostasy. If a church believes that there must be a massive falling away from the faith, then that church avoids partnering with other ministries for fear of contamination. Also, if a church believes that the one world ruler will come and take over a one world government and a one world religion, then all progress toward unity is seen as a supposed sign of the end. Yet, John 17:21-23 and Ephesians 4:11-13 are two very clear passages regarding the Church walking in unity. I am not sure what this will look like, but I believe it still is in our future.

2. Church Grows to Carry the Head

Connected to the mandate of unity is the promise that the Church will mature into a fitting "Body" for Christ as the "Head":

> *And he gave some, apostles; and some, prophets; and some, evangelists; and some, pastors and teachers; For the perfecting of the saints, for the work of the ministry, for the edifying of the body of Christ: Till we all come in the unity of the faith, and of the knowledge of the Son of God, unto a perfect [complete] man, unto the measure of the stature of the fullness of Christ* (Ephesians 4:11-13 NASB).

Throughout the New Testament, the physical body is used as a metaphor to explain the relationship between Christ and His Church. The writers refer to Christ as the "Head" and the Church as His "Body." The passage from Ephesians 4 references this metaphor and declares that the apostles, prophets, evangelists, pastors, and teachers are working toward the goal that the Body of Christ would be *"perfect"* and the *"measure of the stature of Christ."*

Essentially, this is saying that Jesus' Body will someday match His head. Jesus is not going to come back for a weak and sickly body to attach to His head. The Body of Christ will continue to grow and mature, becoming healthy and strong, and then Jesus will have a body capable of carrying His head.

3. The Church Becomes the Mature Bride

The other metaphor that the Bible commonly uses to describe the Church's relationship to Christ is that of a bride and groom:

> *Husbands, love your wives, just as Christ also loved the church and gave Himself for her, that He might sanctify and cleanse her with the washing of water by the word, that He might present her to Himself a glorious church, not having spot or wrinkle or any such thing, but that she should be holy and without blemish* (Ephesians 5:25-27 NKJV).

Jesus is not coming back for a bratty, preteen bride. He is waiting for His bride to come into perfect maturity. The passage in Ephesians 5 shows the balance of timing that is taking place. The bride will not be a small child with spots of food that she has spilled on her dress, neither will she be an old, haggard woman covered with wrinkles. Although 2,000 years of waiting for Christ may seem like a long time, the bride is not old and wrinkly. We are still maturing to the place of being the bride who *"has made herself ready"* (Rev. 19:7). Jesus will return based on the maturity of His beautiful bride. He will not leave us to become old spinsters and He will not come back early before we have been made ready.

4. The Church Brings Forth the Sons of God

The "sons of God" is a term that applies to all who are His children, both male and female. We are the sons of God, and we have a crucial role to fulfill in relation to creation.

> *I consider that the sufferings of this present time are not worthy to be compared with the glory that is to be revealed to us. For the anxious longing of the creation waits eagerly for the revealing of the sons of God. For the creation was subjected to futility, not willingly, but because of Him who subjected it, in hope that the creation itself also will be set free from its slavery to corruption into the freedom of the glory of the children of God* (Romans 8:18-21 NASB).

When we see earthquakes, tsunamis, tornadoes, wildfires, floods, and many other natural disasters, I believe that this is the most important passage to keep in view. Rather than immediately asking, "What sin is God judging?" or, "What gave the devil access to bring such destruction?" or simply concluding (wrongly), "It must be a sign of the times," we can find a better understanding of what is taking place on earth through this passage. The earth is subject to frustration. Romans 8:22 (NKJV) says that *"the whole creation groans."*

The children of God are meant to bring earth into glorious freedom. I believe that the children of God will continue to grow into a greater understanding of their identity, which will result in them living in glorious freedom in a way that has not yet been experienced. Where the Spirit of the Lord is, there is freedom (see 2 Cor. 3:17). Someday in the future, the heart of the Church will be filled with this freedom, and it will impact the entire planet.

In Conclusion

In conclusion, I want to say again that my attempt in this chapter was not to go into great historical depth in exposing heretical concepts concerning end-time theology (as that is a book in the making), but rather to point to where we are today. The Kingdom of God is ever-expanding and growing by its own inherent power:

> *...Indeed, in the whole world [that Gospel] is bearing fruit and still is growing [by its own inherent power], even as it has done among yourselves ever since the day you first heard and came to know and understand the grace of God in truth...* (Colossians 1:6).

The Kingdom came in the manger, was proclaimed by John the Baptist, explained and demonstrated by Jesus, confirmed in the covenant of forgiveness at the Last Supper, established more fully by the finishing of the Old Covenant on the cross, passed to the apostolic ambassadors before His ascension, and grew throughout the Book of Acts to reach the entire inhabited civilized world before the AD 70 destruction removed the Old Covenant ways entirely.

God's Kingdom is here and now. It has been here for 2,000 years. It is growing and will continue to do so. Amen and amen!

CHAPTER 8

GATEWAYS OF THE THREE-DIMENSIONAL NATURE OF HUMANKIND

You are crucified with Christ and free from all of the law's requirements. You can add absolutely nothing to what Jesus Christ has accomplished for you on the Cross of Calvary, and any attempt to do so would be an insult to the Spirit of Grace.

—Jeff Jansen

He saved us, not because of any works of righteousness that we had done, but because of His own pity and mercy, by [the] cleansing [bath] of the new birth (regeneration) and renewing of the Holy Spirit (Titus 3:5).

There has been much confusion to date regarding how a believer walks in the spirit and not in the flesh. Much of this confusion comes from unclear terminology used to describe flesh and spirit. Before we can discuss the subject of being co-crucified with Christ, we must lay a clear foundation of terminology for communicating. I have, with permission, taken sections from Jonathan Welton's book *Eyes of Honor* to help bring clarity into the following portion of this book.

The following are three terms and concepts that must be understood:

1. *Soul* refers to one of the three components that humankind is made of: spirit, soul, and body (1 Thess. 5:21). I agree with the standard definition of the soul as the mind, will, and emotions.
2. *Self* is the word that Jesus used when He referred to denying self. Self is not synonymous with the flesh or the soul. The word "self" is better understood as a person's reputation.
3. The *flesh, fleshly, carnal, carnality, the old nature, and the old man* are synonymous terms that refer to the part of humans that is drawn after and under the influence of sin.

Now that the terms are defined, their usage in God's Word, the Bible, can be properly addressed.

Fighting the Soul

The famous author Watchman Nee caused a lot of confusion regarding these three definitions, especially by teaching that the flesh is comprised of a combination of the soul and the body (in contrast to definitions just given). I will expound more on the vital importance of this subtle definition difference.

I am an admirer of Watchman Nee and have read his books. His book *Spiritual Man* has influenced modern thought toward the soul more than any other. It is with all due respect that I offer a correction on his approach.

I agree with Nee's teaching that the spirit of a believer has been perfected by new birth. However, I disagree with his idea that the soul and body are defined as "the flesh" and are basically evil. This teaching creates a never-ending inward struggle between the soul and the spirit that has become the prevailing mindset of much of the modern church. Yet the Bible does not teach this and it is not an accurate definition of what is considered *the flesh*.

When we are born from above, according to Scripture, the spirit of the person becomes *perfect*, *quickened*, or *made alive* as a new creation in Christ. The Lord never condemned the human soul as an evil thing. In fact, He made the human soul before the fall of humankind: Adam and Eve both had souls. To equate the soul as the flesh is inaccurate. Consider what Jesus said:

> *And you shall love the Lord your God out of and with your whole heart and out of and with all your soul (your life) and out of and with all your mind (with your faculty of thought and your moral understanding) and out of and with all your strength* (Mark 12:30).

If the soul is equal to the carnal nature, how could we possibly love God with our evil flesh?

What Is the Flesh?

Since our *flesh* nature is not composed of the soul or the body, then what is the flesh? The flesh refers to a person's lower nature. This lower nature in Scripture is called *the carnal nature, the flesh, the old nature, the body of death, and the old man*. The flesh is the internal part of humankind that is inclined toward evil desires.

The flesh operates in the realm of human design composed of the soul and body, and every human being has a portion that is inclined toward unhealthy appetites. This is the flesh. As long as we continue to confuse our soul with our flesh, we will continue to fight our own soul as if it were our mortal enemy. The carnal nature is our enemy.

During the early church, the Gnostic's taught that the spirit was good and the physical and emotional realms were evil, and therefore Jesus could not have come to earth in an actual physical body. They taught that Jesus came to earth only as an ethereal spirit being. This teaching is heretical because it negates the truth of Jesus shedding His human blood for the remission of sin. John clearly confronts the heresy of the Gnostics in his early letters because they gained so many followers in the early church.

That which was from the beginning, which we have heard, which we have seen with our eyes, which we have looked at and our hands have touched—this we proclaim concerning the Word of life. The life appeared; we have seen it and testify to it, and we proclaim to you the eternal life, which was with the Father and has appeared to us. We proclaim to you what we have seen and heard, so that you also may have fellowship with us. And our fellowship is with the Father and with his Son, Jesus Christ (1 John 1:1-3 NIV).

John was writing to prove, as an eyewitness, that Jesus was not an ethereal spirit, but a real, physical person. John was the disciple who leaned his head upon Jesus' physical chest at the last supper. He wrote saying that those who claim Jesus didn't have a physical body are actually antichrist.

Dear friends, do not believe every spirit, but test the spirits to see whether they are from God, because many false prophets have gone out into the world. This is how you can recognize the Spirit of God: Every spirit that acknowledges that Jesus Christ has come in the flesh is from God, but every spirit that does not acknowledge Jesus is not from God. This is the spirit of the antichrist, which you have heard is coming and even now is already in the world (1 John 4:1-3 NIV).

While many modern-day Christians believe that the soul and body are evil, the Bible teaches nothing of the sort. The body is actually referred to as the temple of the Holy Spirit (1 Cor. 3:16; 6:19).

Do you not know that your body is a temple of the Holy Spirit…? (1 Corinthians 6:19 NASB)

The soul is never used in the Bible as a negative term. Typically, those who are influenced by Gnostic teachings will refer negatively to things as soulish, of the soul, the soul realm, soul ties, soul power, etc. But biblically speaking, there is nothing inherently evil about the soul. We are not in a battle against our own soul.

There is a struggle against the flesh, but the flesh is not the same as the soul. To follow the Gnostic heresy to its reasonable application, we must: 1) become completely spirit, 2) suppress our soul, or 3) set our spirit against our soul for the rest of our lives. Thankfully, none of these options are true. Your soul is not the flesh, and you never need to crucify your soul.

Gateways of the Three-Dimensional Human Nature

When we come to Christ, we receive a new nature. Our once-dead spirit is made alive in Christ. There is an outer working of the Spirit of God through our spirit that brings transformation within us as we grow and mature in Christ—but we must partner with Him. We must come into agreement with the Spirit of Life in Christ Jesus and all He has done for us on the cross. I love what Pastor Bill Johnson says about the power of the transformed mind, "The Holy Spirit is imprisoned in the bodies of unbelieving believers, and is looking for a way out."

God is looking for a way out of the spirit of man or what I call the *spirit gate*, bringing the power of transformation into the soul and body.

The glory of God enters the spirit of a person as Christ is invited into his or her life as personal Lord and Savior. The Spirit of God brings the power of transformation in and through the soul as we honor, yield, and commune with the Lord through prayer, reverence, faith, hope, worship, and intimacy with Him.

The Spirit of God then begins to paint on the canvas of our mind, bringing transformation to the soul as we yield to Him our conscience, reason, imagination, and mind, which is the conscious, subconscious, unconscious, emotions, and will.

Gateways of the Three-Dimensional Human Nature

The following diagram reveals a simple biblical blueprint for what I believe is the process of transformation in our lives.

Gateways of the Three-Dimensional Nature of Man

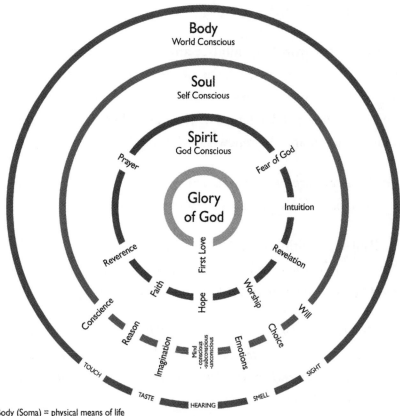

Body (Soma) = physical means of life
Soul (Psyche) = natural life of men; mind, emotions, & will
Spirit (Phneuma) = highest form of life; the very power of life
Glory of God (Zoe) = lives within the spirit of man

We then discern God through our five natural senses in the physical world around us.

But solid food is for full-grown men, for those whose senses and mental faculties are trained by practice to discriminate and distinguish between what is morally good and noble and what is evil and contrary either to divine or human law (Hebrews 5:14).

There is a worrying mindset among many in the body that when Christ comes into us, we are made a completely new creation in Christ not only in spirit, but in the soul and body also. This kind of thinking is dangerous as it seeks to bypass the process of transformation and the renewal of the mind.

And be constantly renewed in the spirit of your mind [having a fresh mental and spiritual attitude] (Ephesians 4:23).

Paul was writing to the church at Ephesus who were Christians. He told them to be *"constantly renewed in the spirit of your mind."* Paul also wrote in his letter to the Romans:

*Do not be conformed to this world (this age), [fashioned after and adapted to its external, superficial customs], but be **transformed (changed) by the [entire] renewal of your mind**...* (Romans 12:2).

Bill Johnson says in his book *The Supernatural Power of a Transformed Mind:*

The "renewed" mind is the canvas on which the Spirit of God can paint." When you came to Christ you did not lose your capacity to sin, but you did lose your capacity to enjoy sinning! You see we still have the capacity to sin and miss the mark, as sin is always a choice. If we are completely new in spirit, soul, and body after coming to Christ as some are supposing, then what was Paul talking about with the process of the renewing of the mind? Scripture does not teach that we are altogether new in soul and body; however it does teach that we are being transformed and are in process of Christ being fully formed in us. Look at what Paul wrote to the Galatian church who he called "little children":

My little children, for whom I am again suffering birth pangs until Christ is completely and permanently formed (molded) within you (Galatians 4:19).

Unity of Spirit, Soul, and Body

There are many things that fascinate me about God, but none come close to the mystery of our identity in Christ. Just thinking that we have been cut out of the same swatch of cloth as God causes me to rush with anticipation. When I think about being alive in eternity before I was born or before the worlds were created, it makes me want to know the reality of that life in eternity. I want to know what it's like and what's happening there.

The reality is, you are spirit. Your spirit came from Heaven and has been in existence a long time. Your spirit has memories of life in Heaven. However, when your spirit came into your body at birth, it became wrapped in the soul and those memories began to fade and were eventually lost.

Before Jesus was born on earth, He was a Spirit. He existed in the bosom of the Father:

No man has ever seen God at any time; the only unique Son, or the only begotten God, Who is in the bosom [in the intimate presence] of the Father, He has declared Him [He has revealed Him and brought Him out where He can be seen; He has interpreted Him and He has made Him known] (John 1:18).

Jesus came to earth as a spirit and lived in a physical body with a soul. Jesus is still Man with spirit, soul, and body, only now He has a resurrected body since He rose from the dead. Yes, we are spirit, but God gave us a soul and body also. We are new creations in Christ.

We are spirit beings, but we are human beings, too. All of our spirit, soul, and body need to come into alignment with the Kingdom of God—this only happens first through the spirit, though. Paul wrote:

Now may the God of peace Himself sanctify you entirely; and may your spirit and soul and body be preserved complete… (1 Thessalonians 5:23 NASB).

It's important that we, as spirit, soul, and body, blend as one so we can interact with both the spiritual and physical realm. Heaven was first a spiritual world. But then God created the earth and brought Heaven into it; He brought Heaven into a physical dimension. When you were born again, Christ came into your spirit, and in that seed is the fullness of the Godhead: Father, Son, and Holy Spirit. You are filled with eternity past, present, and future.

For in Him the whole fullness of Deity (the Godhead) continues to dwell in bodily form [giving complete expression of the divine nature]. And you are in Him, made full and having come to fullness of life [in Christ you too are filled with the

Godhead—Father, Son and Holy Spirit—and reach full spiritual stature]. And He is the Head of all rule and authority [of every angelic principality and power] (Colossians 2:9-10).

But you have an anointing from the Holy One, and you know all things (1 John 2:20 NKJV).

Everything past, present, and future has already been written on the fabric of your spirit. If you come into union with the Holy Spirit, you indeed know all things.

CHAPTER 9

CO-CRUCIFIED WITH CHRIST

Jesus vanquished Satan, not for Himself, but for man. His victory over Satan was purely a substitutionary act. So Christ's victory is our victory. For all that He did in substitution, He did for us. The Supreme Court of the Universe looks upon the substitutionary work of Jesus as though it was actually ours. God did not need it, Jesus did not need it, the angels did not need it, but humanity needed the victory He wrought. God the Father sees Jesus as our perfect Redeemer and us as perfectly redeemed ones. He sees us entering into the fruits of the victory of Jesus, as absolute conquerors over all the forces of darkness.

—E. W. Kenyon

Question and Answer: Are we co-crucified, buried, resurrected, raised, and co-seated with Christ? Absolutely!

We have a new nature in Christ and are provided with all of the supernatural working of the Holy Spirit within us as a new-creation reality. The old *carnal nature* or *flesh* has been put to death, but we must also appropriate the inner working of grace by choosing to cooperate with and walk in the newness of the life of Christ as He is being fully formed and molded within us.

We must choose to put on Christ and stop thinking about the flesh or indulging the lower nature. Starve it. The grace and power of God by virtue of rebirth is within you.

> *But clothe yourself with the Lord Jesus Christ (the Messiah), and make no provision for [indulging] the flesh [put a stop to thinking about the evil cravings of your physical nature] to [gratify its] desires (lusts)* (Romans 13:14).

Our Flesh Was Crucified with Christ

I have already been co-crucified with Christ: nevertheless I ever live yet no longer I, but Christ ever lives in me: and the life I now ever live in the flesh, I ever live in faith by the Son of God, who once then having loved me, also at intervals is giving Himself up (Galatians 2:20 Expanded Greek Translation (EGT)).

Co-crucified is a verb in the perfect tense in the Greek text indicating that it is already completely done. As a result, it is impossible for us to add anything to this completely finished work by anything that we should do today. Our old self, the old nature, was co-crucified with Him in order that the body of sin might then be *rendered powerless,* and that "we are no longer to continually serve sin" (Rom. 6:6 EGT). The Greek word for "rendered powerless" in this verse is *katargethe,* which means to be *unemployed.* The old self is *put out of work, rendered powerless, unemployed* in us.

Sin problems in born-again believers are not the primary issues. The focus for the reborn into a new nature in Christ is the revelation needed to render sin powerless as we walk in that truth. We need this Holy Spirit revelation.

When Jesus died on the cross, He not only took our sinful actions upon Himself, He also took our flesh nature upon Himself.

Remember: the *flesh* refers to a person's lower nature, which in scripture is also called *the carnal nature, the flesh, the old nature, the body of death, and the old man*. The flesh is the internal part of mankind that is inclined toward evil desires. We have thereby been crucified with Christ.

> *For Christ's love compels us, because we are convinced that one died for all, and therefore all died. And he died for all, that those who live should no longer live for themselves but for him who died for them and was raised again* (2 Corinthians 5:14-15 NIV).

> *I have been crucified with Christ and I no longer live, but Christ lives in me. The life I now live in the body, I live by faith in the Son of God, who loved me and gave himself for* (Galatians 2:20 NIV).

What? Crucify Ourselves?

The majority of the church believes that Jesus crucified our flesh, but that we also are in a process of crucifying our flesh. Yet the Bible does not teach us to crucify ourselves. Our crucifixion in Christ was done in the past and we cannot add anything to what Christ has done for us.

Unfortunately, some Bible translations do not translate accurately the verb tenses regarding our crucifixion, but the original manuscripts of the New Testament are consistent. Every verse regarding our crucifixion in Christ speaks of it as past tense; never present or future.

The following are some past-tense examples:

Those who belong to Christ Jesus have crucified the flesh with its passions and desires (Galatians 5:24 NIV).

In him you were also circumcised with a circumcision not performed by human hands. Your whole self ruled by the flesh was put off when you were circumcised by Christ (Colossians 2:11 NIV).

For you died, and your life is now hidden with Christ in God (Colossians 3:3 NIV).

Therefore consider the members of your earthly body as dead to immorality, impurity, passion, evil desire, and greed, which amounts to idolatry (Colossians 3:5 NASB).

Do not lie to each other, since you have taken off your old self with its practices (Colossians 3:9 NIV).

Therefore, if anyone is in Christ, he is a new creation; old things have passed away; behold, all things have become new (2 Corinthians 5:17 NKJV).

But as for you, not in this manner did you learn the Christ, since, indeed, as is the case, you heard and in Him were taught just as truth is in Jesus, that you have put off once for all with reference to your former manner of life the old self who is being corrupted according to the passionate desires of deceit; moreover, that you are being constantly renewed with reference to the spirit of your mind; and that you have put on once for all the new self who after God was created in righteousness and holiness of truth (Ephesians 4:20-24 Kenneth Wuest Translation).

By no means! We are those who have died to sin; how can we live in it any longer? Or don't you know that all of us who were baptized into Christ Jesus were baptized into his death? We were therefore buried with him through baptism into death in order that, just as Christ was raised from the dead through the glory of the Father, we too may live a new life (Romans 6:2-4 NIV).

It Is Finished

Jesus completed His mission on the Cross of Calvary and it is finished. Christ has done it, and He did it all for our benefit. We can rest knowing that Jesus did for us what we were powerless to accomplish on our own.

There remains therefore a rest for the people of God. For he who has entered His rest has himself also ceased from his works as God did from His (Hebrews 4:9-10 NKJV).

Jesus has ceased from His work and is sitting at the Father's right hand in a place of rest.

But this Man, after He had offered one sacrifice for sins forever, sat down at the right hand of God, from that time waiting till His enemies are made His footstool (Hebrews 10:12-13).

Jesus is resting until the Father puts all His enemies under His feet. As we take our place in Him and enter into His rest, we also invite the Father to put our enemies under our feet as well. He is the Head and we are His Body. The Father will subdue all things under our feet in Christ. This is not a passive place of being, but rather an active cooperation with God. From our place of enthronement with Him, we exercise godly dominion in partnership with Him.

Sink into Your New Self

Not only does the Word direct us to *put off* certain things, but there are also many things that Scripture tells us to *put on*. Many Christians have taken the phrase *put on* and have tried to use it as a formula. For example, there are those who daily declare, "I choose today to put on the armor of God." They work and work, trying to put on the new self, but this was not the intention of the New Testament writers when they said put on the new nature:

> *and to put on the new self, created to be like God in true righteousness and holiness* (Ephesians 4:24 NIV).

> *and having put on the new self, which is being renewed in knowledge in the image of its Creator* (Colossians 3:10 NIV).

The New Testament phrase *put on* comes from the Greek root word *enduo,* which means to sink into. *Putting on* Christ does not mean that we must work and strive in human efforts. Putting on Christ means to *sink into* or lean back and rest in our identity in Christ.

> *The night is nearly over; the day is almost here. So let us put aside the deeds of darkness and put on the armor of light* (Romans 13:12 NIV).

and to put on the new self, created to be like God in true righteousness and holiness (Ephesians 4:24).

Put on the full armor of God, so that you can take your stand against the devil's schemes (Ephesians 6:11 NIV).

Therefore put on the full armor of God, so that when the day of evil comes, you may be able to stand your ground, and after you have done everything, to stand (Ephesians 6:13 NIV).

and have put on the new self, which is being renewed in knowledge in the image of its Creator (Colossians 3:10 NIV).

And over all these virtues put on love, which binds them all together in perfect unity (Colossians 3:14).

The *putting on* that Paul talks about in Scripture is not based in striving, but rather sinking into the provision of grace and our new life in Christ. This is incredible news for those who have been working hard to die to themselves and crucify their flesh daily. How liberating it is to receive Christ's accomplished work on our behalf and to believe in our new nature. Once you see that the battle against your flesh and sin nature is actually a mirage, you will be empowered to *put off* the garment of your old nature and begin living according to the new.

CHAPTER 10

SECRETS OF THE ASCENDED LIFE

The Resurrection of the Lord Jesus is the proof of Satan's defeat, of man's Redemption, and of God's legal right to make the believer a New Creation. God has lifted the believer above all rule and authority and power and dominion, not only in this age, but in that which is to come. He put all things in subjection under the believer's feet. He gave Christ who is the head of the body to be master over all the forces of the universe.

—*E. W. Kenyon*

We cannot claim any blessing that is not plainly proclaimed in God's Word. Faith begins where the will of God is known. God's Word reveals God's will. First, notice Paul's description of Christ's resurrection in the chapter of his letter to the Ephesians:

And what is the exceeding greatness of His power in us who believe, according to the working of His mighty power which

He worked in Christ when He raised Him from the dead and enthroned Him at His right hand in the heavenly places, far above all principality and power and might and dominion, and every name that is named, not only in this age but also in that which is to come (Ephesians 1:19-21 NKJV).

Paul informs us that the power that is working in us is the same power that raised Christ from the dead and enthroned Him at the Father's right hand. Christ is enthroned far above all other spiritual beings that exist in the heavenly realms. As Paul continues in his letter to the Ephesians, he writes:

But God, who is rich in mercy, because of His great love with which He loved us, even when we were dead in trespasses, made us alive together with Christ (by grace you have been saved), and raised us up together, and made us sit together in the heavenly places in Christ Jesus (Ephesians 2:4-6 NKJV).

In raising Christ from the dead, the apostle saw by revelation that we were raised with Him and enthroned with Him at the Father's right hand. We are enthroned with Him in the higher realm of heavenly places far above principalities and power and every name that is named (see Eph. 1:21). It is important to note that in the unseen realm of spiritual reality, we are enthroned above all other spiritual beings.

Paul uses the phrase *heavenly places* five times in the Book of Ephesians:

Blessed be the God and Father of our Lord Jesus Christ, who has blessed us with every spiritual blessing in the heavenly places in Christ (Ephesians 1:3 NKJV).

which He worked in Christ when He raised Him from the dead and seated Him at His right hand in the heavenly places (Ephesians 1:20 NKJV).

and raised us up together, and made us sit together in the heavenly places in Christ Jesus (Ephesians 2:6 NKJV).

to the intent that now the manifold wisdom of God might be made known through the church to the principalities and powers in the heavenly places (Ephesians 3:10 NKJV).

For we do not wrestle against flesh and blood, but against principalities, against powers, against the rulers of the darkness of this age, against spiritual hosts of wickedness in the heavenly places (Ephesians 6:12 NKJV).

Apparently, the realm of heavenly places contains both a higher and a lower realm. The evil hosts of wickedness are in the heavenly realms, but Christ is enthroned far above them, and we are in Him. Our co-enthroning with Christ is far above these other spiritual beings. We are blessed with every spiritual blessing in this realm. Our warfare against the principalities and powers is from our position above them. They attempt to bring us down from our position of absolute victory by deceiving us into fighting on their level. It is the destiny of the Church to demonstrate the many-sided wisdom of God to these very principalities and powers (see Eph. 3:10).

As our minds are renewed and our faith grows, we take these realities as fact and live in the light of them. We come to know that we are above our enemies and refuse to walk in the flesh realm, taking our place in Christ in the spirit realm. The following is an excerpt from Pastor John G. Lake's article *The Power of the Name:*

The miracle realm is man's natural realm. He is by creation the companion of the miracle-working God. Sin dethroned man from the miracle-working realm, but through grace he is coming into his own. In the beginning, man's spirit was the dominant force in the world; when he sinned his mind became dominant. Sin dethroned the spirit and crowned the intellect. But grace is restoring the spirit to its place of dominion, and when man comes to realize this, he will live in the realm of the supernatural without effort. No longer will faith be a struggle, but a normal living in the realm of God. The spiritual realm places men where communion with God is a normal experience. Miracles are then his native breath.

Reality of Ascended Living

The reality of our new life in Christ requires a renewing of our minds. What the Father says is divine fact. The declarations of God are the highest form of reality other than God Himself. The creative ability of God was released when He spoke all matter into being. And in the eternal purpose of God, the first creation becomes the type of the *new creation*.

> *For it is the God who commanded light to shine out of darkness, who has shone in our hearts to give the light of the knowledge of the glory of God in the face of Jesus Christ* (2 Corinthians 4:6 NKJV).

Father has commanded light to shine into our darkness and impart the knowledge of the glory of God. He has declared us to be raised and enthroned with Christ at His right hand. As we embrace these truths, the Holy Spirit bears witness with our spirits that we are indeed sons and daughters of God and joint heirs with Christ.

> *But to as many as did receive and welcome Him, He gave the authority (power, privilege, right) to become the children of God, that is, to those who believe in (adhere to, trust in, and rely on) His name—who owe their birth neither to [a]bloods nor to the will of the flesh [that of physical impulse] nor to the will of man [that of a natural father], but to God. [They are born of God!]* (John 1:12-13).

We Are Seated in Heavenly Places

The more we meditate on the revelation of enthronement, the more we accept and believe it, the more that place gets on us. Heavenly encounters increase and angelic activity abounds. Every spiritual blessing has been given to us in the heavenly places (see Eph. 1:3). We are not going to grovel in the earthly realm because we are seated in the heavenly places with the Lord. Every believer has the right, authority, and ability to minister out of the Throne Room, just as Jesus did.

The Church is entering a time when we won't want anything but the very heart and mind of the Father. We are going through a transformation that we must embrace, as Paul stresses:

> *In Him we preach, warning every man and teaching every man in all wisdom, that we may present every man perfect in Christ Jesus. To this end I also labor, striving according to His working which works in me mightily* (Colossians 1:28-29 NKJV).

The question is, are you hungry for transformation? I know I am. I want to know, hear, see, and be like Jesus. Embrace His work in you so that He can work through you mightily. Embrace the ministry of the Holy Spirit and allow the sevenfold flow of the Holy Spirit to manifest in your life.

As we understand our divine union with Him and become obedient to His voice, we can engage face to Face, spirit to Spirit, and unite our hearts to His. When we plug in to the center pipe of the heavenly menorah, we receive the fresh oil of Psalm 92:10: *"I am anointed with fresh oil."*

As the fresh oil pours in from the Word, the anointing pours into the vat and we become partakers of that rich flow of the unlimited anointing and union of the Holy Spirit.

Fresh oil feeds the flames—the seven flames atop the seven pipes. It has to be a continuous flow of oil for the seven flames to burn. We trim the wick and replenish the oil in perpetual communion with Him, and the flame burns in divine union with Him. The greater the flow of oil, the greater the flame. The greater the flame, the greater the favor and influence.

Keys to Living the Ascended Life

In this section, I give some keys that will help you develop a lifestyle of ascended living. One of the greatest keys I've come to know is the Kingdom principal of *beholding and becoming.* I also call this the Kingdom Law of Focus. You become what you set your attention upon. Proverbs 23:7 says: *"For as he thinks in his heart, so is he."*

In other words, whatever I set my gaze upon is what I become. Personally, I've found this to be one of the most important keys to living the ascended life. Paul wrote to the Colossian church and encouraged them to:

> *Set your mind* [attention] *on things above, not on things on the earth* (Colossians 3:2 NKJV).

Beholding and Becoming

Paul, in his letter to the Corinthian church, revealed this amazing truth about beholding and becoming:

But we all, with unveiled face, beholding as in a mirror the glory of the Lord, are being transformed into the same image from glory to glory, just as by the Spirit of the Lord (2 Corinthians 3:18 NKJV).

When we behold the Lord as in a mirror we are being transformed into the same image. As we stare or gaze upon the Lord, the law of focus brings the intimate union of our spirit into an unbroken union with Jesus Himself.

I've been swept away into the Throne Room in this type of trans-like meditation. The word used for "transformation" here is the Greek word *metamorphoo*, where we get the word metamorphosis. It means to literally be transfigured. The same word is used when Jesus was transfigured in Mark 9 on the mountain where He was with Peter, James, and John.

Six days after this, Jesus took with Him Peter and James and John and led them up on a high mountain apart by themselves. And He was transfigured before them and became resplendent with divine brightness. And His garments became glistening, intensely white, as no fuller (cloth dresser, launderer) on earth could bleach them. And Elijah appeared [there] to them, accompanied by Moses, and they were holding [a protracted] conversation with Jesus (Mark 9:2-4).

Jesus was transfigured before them. He was changed, morphed; it's an inward molecular change. We can have the radiant glory of

God shining from every part of us. In the process of beholding and becoming through intimate union with Jesus Himself, Peter says we become partakers of the divine nature.

By means of these He has bestowed on us His precious and exceedingly great promises, so that through them you may escape [by flight] from the moral decay (rottenness and corruption) that is in the world because of covetousness (lust and greed), and become sharers (partakers) of the divine nature (2 Peter 1:4).

Soaking in the Secret Place

Jesus told us to go into our prayer closets and close the door behind us, so we could pray to our Father in secret.

But when you pray, go into your [most] private room, and, closing the door, pray to your Father, Who is in secret; and your Father, Who sees in secret, will reward you in the open (Matthew 6:6).

Soaking prayer is the door that opens the eternal realm of Heaven in our lives and releases the knowledge of the glory of the Lord in the earth.

Key Scripture Passages

[For my determined purpose is] that I may know Him [that I may progressively become more deeply and intimately acquainted with Him, perceiving and recognizing and understanding the wonders of His Person more strongly and more clearly].... I press on toward the goal to win the [supreme and heavenly] prize to which God in Christ Jesus is calling us upward (Philippians 3:10-14).

He who dwells in the secret place of the Most High shall remain stable and fixed under the shadow of the Almighty [Whose power no foe can withstand] (Psalm 91:1).

Be still, and know that I am God... (Psalm 46:10 NKJV).

And do not be drunk with wine...but be filled with the Spirit (Ephesians 5:18 NKJV).

...He will baptize you with the Holy Spirit and fire (Matthew 3:11 NKJV).

...For indeed, the kingdom of God is within you (Luke 17:21 NKJV).

And He raised us up together with Him and made us sit down together [giving us joint seating with Him] in the heavenly sphere [by virtue of our being] in Christ Jesus (the Messiah, the Anointed One) (Ephesians 2:6).

If then you have been raised with Christ [to new life, thus sharing His resurrection from the dead], aim at and seek the [rich, eternal treasures] that are above, where Christ is, seated at the right hand of God. And set your minds and keep them set on what is above (the higher things), not on the things that are on the earth. For [as far as this world is concerned] you have died, and your [new, real] life is hidden with Christ in God (Colossians 3:1-3).

...let us run with endurance the race that is set before us, fixing our eyes on Jesus, the author and perfecter of faith, who for the joy set before Him endured the cross, despising the shame, and

has sat down at the right hand of the throne of God (Hebrews 12:1-2 NASB).

What Do You Mean, "Soaking"?

Soaking in the secret place of His presence is a form a prayer, but not the type that probably comes to mind. Prayer in the Western world often looks like a lot of rambling, a lot of asking God for something, and a lot of "religious duty." Soaking prayer actually has very little to do with talking to God and more to do with listening to Him. Soaking is posturing yourself in a place to receive from God after giving Him all of yourself. Soaking is positioning yourself in a place of stillness and quietness. It is a place of meditation and contemplation on the Person of Jesus Christ and the indwelling presence of the Holy Spirit—this is a place of genuine, internal peace and rest.

The reason we use the word "soaking" when referring to this type of prayer comes from the Greek word *baptizmo*, which is where we get the English word "baptize." John the Baptist said:

> *I indeed baptize you in (with) water because of repentance [that is, because of your changing your minds for the better, heartily amending your ways, with abhorrence of your past sins]. But He Who is coming after me is mightier than I, Whose sandals I am not worthy or fit to take off or carry; He will baptize you with the Holy Spirit and with fire* (Matthew 3:11).

John stated that he baptized in water, but that Jesus would baptize us in the Holy Spirit and fire. The Greek word *baptizmo* means "to dip." It contains all of the following meanings: to dip repeatedly, immersing, fully submerging (as in a sinking ship), washing or bathing oneself, and overwhelming.

We want to be soaked, fully submerged, repeatedly dipped, washed, bathed, overwhelmed, and consumed with the presence of the Holy Spirit. Like a dry and brittle sponge needs to be dipped in water, we need to be fully submerged and baptized in the river of God's presence until every fiber of our being is filled to overflowing so we leak and spill out the glory of God everywhere we go.

There are two primary Hebrew words translated into the English word "anoint" in the Old Testament: the first word means "to rub," and the second word means "to smear." In both cases, it's talking about rubbing or smearing oil.

The anointing of God is like oil: it's tangible, transferable, and when not properly contained, it has a tendency to get all over everything. Remember, it's the Person of the Holy Spirit who carries the anointing and power of God. When we spend time with Him in the presence of Jesus Christ, the Anointed One, we can't help but have the anointing of God rubbed and smeared deep into our lives and ministries. It gets all over everything. Jesus said that we would be baptized in the Holy Spirit:

> *For John baptized with water, but not many days from now you shall be baptized with (placed in, introduced into) the Holy Spirit* (Acts 1:5).

Jesus said we would be baptized, smeared, soaked, and completely submerged in the Holy Spirit. Soaking is actually like pickling. You take a cucumber, soak it in vinegar and spices, and over time it turns into a pickle. We want to go into God's presence as a cucumber and come out like a juicy dill. We need to be pickled in the presence of God. Paul says in Ephesians 5:18 (NASB) not to *"get drunk with wine, for that is dissipation, but be filled with the Spirit."* The words, "be filled," in this verse denote multiple and continual infillings of the Holy Spirit. Paul is saying that being filled with the Holy Spirit is not a one-time event. In the Greek, it actually means, "be being filled," or a continual infilling and submerging in the presence of God.

There are many ministers of the Gospel who have been released into ministry or have had a major breakthrough in their ministry after a season of soaking and ministering to the Lord in the secret place. This was the case for me.

The Visitation

Several years ago, I entered a season of soaking and pressing hard into the Lord. I spent hours in the glory of God, and I was lifted into His presence. Often, while going to bed, I meditated on the presence of God and I extended myself into the Throne Room, ministering to the Lord until I fell asleep. On several occasions, the Lord entered my room and sat at the end of my bed to spend time with me. Other times the glory of God came over the top of my head as a lamp or a ball of light.

During this season, I received many breakthroughs and encounters in the glory of God, but what was about to happen changed my life and ministry forever. After prayer one night, I remember going to bed early because at the time I was both working and ministering to make ends meet. With my eyes closed and the lights off in the bedroom, the light from the glory of God was so intense that my whole body shook as waves of God's love rippled over me—it was pure ecstasy!

That night I was awakened at 11:22 P.M. by the blast of a trumpet. Two angels with long, silver trumpets were standing at the foot of my bed, blowing an alarm in my ears. I felt like John's description on the Island of Patmos when he said that he fell like a dead man (see Rev. 1:17). The fear of the Lord filled my body, and I was completely undone in the hands of God.

The angel on my left blew a trumpet in my left ear. This is what woke me up. The angel on the right was blowing his trumpet in my right ear. What came out, however, wasn't sound, but a hot wind that entered my body and went down into my chest and spirit, then exploded in electric power. Immediately, I was pulled out of my body, through the roof, through the atmosphere, and through the stars, and I came to rest in a large room in Heaven called the Room of Intercession.

I remember thinking that it must have been a dream. As I looked around I saw men, women, children, and angels all praying over the nations. I saw regions of the earth flash before me in a moment of time. Everything was so surreal that I could scarcely take in what I was seeing. In the experience, I looked around and saw myself lying on the floor, yet I was standing above myself at the same time.

As I was watching myself, praise began to flow from my spirit. When you encounter the presence of God, what is in your heart begins to rise to the surface. I began to worship Him saying, "Lord, You're so awesome…so beautiful…Jesus, You're so wonderful and incredible…" This praise was coming out of my mouth, but I noticed two voices were coming out of me. There was my voice, and the voice of the Holy Spirit—both voices were harmoniously singing and declaring the goodness of the Lord.

This encounter lasted through the evening and into the morning. When I awoke, my eyes were opened to a whole new dimension in the Spirit. I was prolifically seeing angels, beings, and shafts of light that moved through the house like colorful, super-natural pathways reaching from my living room into the heavens. My spirit had awakened to a brand-new place in the glory of

God. Rainbows appeared in meetings, and clouds of glory would manifest as I preached. Miracles exploded in the atmosphere with tangible signs of the glory. Often fireballs or honey wheels were released in meetings, and the whole house would be whacked under the power of God. We saw gold teeth, gold dust, gemstones, and other wonderful signs with many healings and creative miracles.

God shifted me, the ministry, and our lives—we've never been the same. I believe God granted this encounter because I hungered and thirsted for Him with my entire being. It wouldn't have happened unless I learned to position myself in a place of stillness, rest, and meditation on the goodness of God. Soaking is a key component to receiving breakthrough in your life and ministry. The breakthrough is the result of a heart sold out to Him.

The Upward Call and Tabernacling with God

[For my determined purpose is] that I may know Him [that I may progressively become more deeply and intimately acquainted with Him, perceiving and recognizing and understanding the wonders of His Person more strongly and more clearly].... I press on toward the goal to win the [supreme and heavenly] prize to which God in Christ Jesus is calling us upward (Philippians 3:10,14).

The whole purpose of soaking, and the entirety of Christianity for that matter, is to walk in a love relationship with Jesus Christ by getting to know Him, His character, and His nature. Throughout Paul's epistles we see a golden thread—a unique strand—that tied all of his writings together. This golden thread is the upward call of God in Christ Jesus. In other words, it's being heavenly minded, and setting our minds, hearts, and affections on things above where

Christ is seated and where we are seated with Him in the heavenly realm. The author of Hebrews tells us:

Let us then fearlessly and confidently and boldly draw near to the throne of grace (the throne of God's unmerited favor to us sinners), that we may receive mercy [for our failures] and find grace to help in good time for every need [appropriate help and well-timed help, coming just when we need it] (Hebrews 4:16).

God has also planted eternity in our hearts and minds.

He has made everything beautiful in its time. He has also set eternity in the human heart; yet no one can fathom what God has done from beginning to end (Ecclesiastes 3:11 NIV).

Ecstatic Prophetic Encounters

Both Isaiah and Ezekiel had incredible Throne Room encounters (see Is. 6:1-13; Ezek. 1:26-28). What they saw was beautiful and amazing, yet their understanding and perception was only in part because they didn't know Christ. John the Revelator was a man like us—a born-again, Spirit-filled believer. Something about Heaven and the realm of eternity seized his being. When banished to the Island of Patmos, John was given a great opportunity to get to know the resurrected Christ even more. I can imagine him praying and pressing in and worshipping God in the Spirit. Undoubtedly, he had read of Isaiah's and Ezekiel's Throne Room encounters and was longing for his own. Then finally, he hears a trumpet and a voice, and is sucked up into the heavenlies to have one of the most amazing encounters ever recorded.

Isaiah and Ezekiel saw dimly the throne and the One who sat upon the throne. John saw the same thing, yet he received a greater unfolding of the revelation of the glory of the Lord. Likewise, when we encounter God on His throne, He can reveal different aspects, characteristics, and revelations of His Person and glory.

Paul had a similar experience:

True, there is nothing to be gained by it, but [as I am obliged] to boast, I will go on to visions and revelations of the Lord. I know a man in Christ who fourteen years ago—whether in the body or out of the body I do not know, God knows—was caught up to the third heaven. And I know that this man— whether in the body or away from the body I do not know, God knows as caught up into paradise, and he heard utterances beyond the power of man to put into words, which man is not permitted to utter. Of this same [man's experiences I will boast, but of myself (personally) I will not boast, except as regards my infirmities (my weaknesses). Should I desire to boast, I shall not be a witless braggart, for I shall be speaking the truth. But I abstain [from it] so that no one may form a higher estimate of me than [is justified by] what he sees in me or hears from me (2 Corinthians 12:1-6).*

Paul and John were both caught up and saw the throne in paradise in the third heaven. John was able to write down the experience, which became the Book of Revelation. Paul, on the other hand, was only permitted to speak of the experience to a degree—seemingly for the purpose of staying humble. Paul and John's ministries and callings were different. John was not only permitted to share what he saw, but he was also commanded to write it down.

Paul's calling was different: he was heavily involved with the Body of Christ, church politics, growth, dos and don'ts, etc. Even though Paul wasn't permitted to publicly share his experience, the revelations from his third heaven encounter obviously leaked out through his life and in all of his ministry and writings.

Our aim is to know God as intimately as He can be known. The only thing that will quench the thirst for eternity in our hearts is if we respond to the invitation to go up the mountain of the Lord to meet with Him. We must, individually and corporately, behold the Lord in all of His glory. When we do this—when we are lifted into His presence—His presence comes down.

When we spend time in Heaven, Heaven comes to earth. When our praises go up, His glory comes down. The more time we spend wrapped in the secret place, the more we will drip Heaven's presence everywhere we walk on this earth. We become a conduit—a glory dispenser. When we go up to make our home with Him, He comes down to make His home with us. I want God to make His home with me. I want Him to dwell, settle down, rest, and abide in my life. I want Him to tabernacle with me—I want to be His tabernacle.

Jesus says:

If a person [really] loves Me, he will keep My word [obey My teaching]; and My Father will love him, and We will come to him and make Our home (abode, special dwelling place) with him (John 14:23).

God has always wanted to make His tabernacle on the earth. This was His original intention in The Garden of Eden, and this will be the grand finale told in Revelation 21:3 (NIV):

"Look! God's dwelling place is now among the people, and he will dwell with them. They will be his people, and God himself will be with them and be their God."

How to Be Still and Know—Entering into Rest

He says, "Be still, and know that I am God" (Psalm 46:10).

The word "still" means idle, quiet, and alone. In this verse, the word "know" takes several phrases to explain the full meaning: come to know by experience, perceive, find, see, be made known, become known, be revealed, and cause to know.

The psalmist David was the master of the *selah*. That word signifies rest. It means to pause and calmly think and meditate in a place of rest and peace. I can see David journaling psalm after psalm and worshipping God. Then he takes a *selah*—he pauses and meditates. When he receives more revelation, he began writing again. When finished, he would pause and take another *selah* until he received more revelation. I think he used it as a means of divine listening.

In the same way, I came to a level of understanding of the Person of God that brought breakthrough in my ministry—all from practicing *selah,* or divine listening.

For he who has once entered [God's] rest also has ceased from [the weariness and pain] of human labors, just as God rested from those labors peculiarly His own. Let us therefore be zealous and exert ourselves and strive diligently to enter that rest [of God, to know and experience it for ourselves], that no one may fall or perish by the same kind of unbelief and disobedience [into which those in the wilderness fell (Hebrews 4:10-11).

And to whom did He swear that they should not enter His rest, but to those who disobeyed [who had not listened to His word and who refused to be compliant or be persuaded]? So we see that they were not able to enter [into His rest], because of their

*unwillingness to adhere to and trust in and rely on God [unbe-
lief had shut them out]* (Hebrews 3:18-19).

*Through these he has given us his very great and precious prom-
ises, so that through them you may participate in the divine
nature, having escaped the corruption in the world caused by
evil desires* (2 Peter 1:4 NIV).

Contemplative Prayer

Contemplative prayer is essentially coming out of the distractions
of the world and into a quiet place of rest and intimacy with the
Lord. In that place, your nature and His nature become one, and
an intimacy is experienced that goes way beyond words. In this
atmosphere, you simply allow your heart to be laid bare and you
allow the dew of Heaven, the very essence of God, to permeate
your spirit, soul, and body. Brother Lawrence probably demonstrated this best through his attempts at "practicing His presence."

Webster's Dictionary and I define "contemplate" as: 1) To
gaze at intensely, reading the Word out loud, quietly, and listening
carefully; 2) To think about intensely; to study, responding to the
Word with your heart and mind; 3) To expect or intend; to meditate, muse; to think or consider deeply; recollecting yourself with
meditation.

A Common, Contemplative Prayer Model

1. Recollecting

Most often, "recollect" means to remember, but it also means to
compose or gather. First, let go of everything but the "here and
now." Realize that God is present here and now. Cast all your anxieties on Him because He cares for you. Practice the presence of

God in the room with you in the moment. Use your imagination to picture the cloud of God's presence wrapping around you. It's not "New Age," but a good use of God's gift of imagination (for example, parables).

2. Prayer of Quiet

At the center of your being you are hushed. You have entered into a listening stillness. All the outward and inward distractions have been silenced and your spirit is completely engaged and on alert to hear and experience God. Bask in the warmth of His presence and simply behold Him.

3. Ecstasy

The Greek word is *ekstasis*, which is most often translated as trance. This state of being is granted by the Lord Himself and cannot be achieved by your own efforts. It is a state of being completely unaware of your surroundings and totally caught up with the Lord.

Six Ingredients of the Contemplative State

1. Physical Calm (Hebrews 4:9-11; Hebrews 3:18-19)
2. Focused Attention (Hebrews 12:1-2; John 5:19)
3. Letting Be (Psalm 46:10; Philippians 4:6-7)
4. Receptivity (John 15:4-5)
5. Spontaneous Flow (John 7:38-39)
6. Beholding (2 Corinthians 3:18)

Advanced Contemplative Prayer Model

Another contemplative prayer model begins the same as before but adds a fourth step:

1. Reflection/Recollecting

Reflection is letting go of everything but God. It's laying aside your past—all of your victories and defeats—and your future—all of your desires and concerns. It's meditating on God in the here and now. To reflect means to cast all anxieties on Him.

Practice the presence of God in the room with you in the moment, and the inward presence of the Holy Spirit—Christ in you—the hope of glory. The entire Kingdom of Heaven resides in your spirit. It's okay to turn inward to hear the voice of God. Again, you can use your imagination to picture the cloud of God's presence wrapping around you. God gave the imagination to you; use it as a tool to engage Heaven. Jesus taught in parables and engaged people's imaginations in order to lead them into a deeper walk with God.

2. Prayer of Quiet

At the center of your being you are hushed. You have entered into a listening stillness. All the outward and inward distractions have been silenced and your spirit is completely engaged and on alert to hear and experience God. Bask in the warmth of His presence and simply behold Him.

3. Ecstasy

The Greek word is *ekstasis*, which is most often translated as trance. This state of being is granted by the Lord himself and cannot be achieved by your own efforts. It is a state of being completely unaware of your surroundings and totally caught up with the Lord.

4. Becoming Completely Still and Beholding Him in all of His Glory

Coming to a place of total stillness during prayer is a great challenge. If you are going to commune with God, first you must become still. Habakkuk went to his guard post to pray (see Hab. 2:1). In the early morning, when it was still dark, Jesus departed to a lonely place to pray (see Mark 1:35). After an entire day filled with ministry, Jesus went to a mountain to pray. Stillness is not necessarily the goal. It's a means to go deeper with God. It is the door in which we are able to fellowship and commune with the Lord, spirit to Spirit.

Coming to a place of total stillness cannot be hurried, forced, or accomplished because of your ability or self-effort; rather, it must be allowed to happen. At a point in your stillness, God begins to take over, and you sense His active flow within you. At this point, spontaneous images begin to flow with a life of their own. He speaks, and you hear. He imparts supernatural strength, wisdom, and endowments in this place of stillness.

Dealing with Distractions

1. Outward Distractions

There are many outward distractions that could pull you away from pressing into God. If you're at your house, it could be the phone, neighbors, pets, kids, chores, cleaning, unwanted guests, email, texting, television, etc. At first, when practicing the presence of God, it may be necessary to eliminate outward distractions as much as possible. It's also helpful to set aside time every day, normally the same time every day, to pray, meditate, and practice soaking. This helps develop a pattern and a discipline for feasting on God's presence. Later, after doing this for a while, you will learn to carry the same presence of God, that you experience during your soaking sessions, into the workplace, school, grocery store, etc. You become a bearer of His glory and power when you learn to stay in the secret place while doing everyday tasks. This happens through continual worship, prayer, adoration, and beholding Him.

2. Inward Distractions

For most people, inward distractions are a little more difficult to take care of than the outward type. When I'm pressing in, and all I can think about is my "to-do" list, I've found it helpful to take a minute to write down all the things I need to accomplish. This helps remove it from my mind and subconscious because I can refer back to the list later. If you feel a block because of some type of sin, or you're very sin-conscious, confess it, repent, get rid of it, and keep moving forward. It has been nailed to the cross—if you've confessed and God has forgiven you, you must forgive yourself too. If you find that your mind wanders aimlessly, it's helpful to speak in tongues, sing and worship, focus on Jesus, and meditate on the Word until your mind becomes still.

Levels of Ascension

We need to remember one thing: the level of ascension that we enter into with the Lord will determine the level of miracles we will see manifest in our own personal ministries. If the ascent isn't high enough, it will make the difference between migraines being healed, or body parts being recreated. There are times in our personal lives and meetings that there's been no atmosphere, no sense of the presence of God, or no ascension into His presence. The secret to ascending higher in the glory of God is personal and corporate praise. You praise, praise, PRAISE…until you get the breakthrough.

How long should it take for you to walk into a meeting and be in the presence of God? Immediately. Is it the number of songs you sing? No, it's not. Some of the songs we sing never quite get us to where we need to be in the Spirit. High praise is what brings you before the face of God.

I don't want to just come occasionally before the face of God, or live at a low or medium level of glory, I want to live in the very presence of God, continually as Enoch did.

CHAPTER 11

THRONE ROOM FREQUENCIES

Just as there are two forms of light, natural and supernatural, so there are two different frequencies of sound, the sound of Heaven and the sound of the earth. The sounds of earth have been influenced and are cluttered with human and demonic debris that can only be changed by the spoken Word in the Holy Spirit. These dark, earthly sounds carry a frequency or vibration that works against our spirits, souls, and bodies to break them down spiritually and molecularly in order to imprison them. Satan is known as the "prince of the power of the air" in Ephesians 2:2, and his attempt is to keep us from harmony with the voice of the God. But we must rise above the noise and debris of the world and ascend into the new sounds of Heaven in the Throne Room. Isaiah 60:1-3 says:

Arise [from the depression and prostration in which circum-stances have kept you—rise to a new life]! Shine (be radiant with the glory of the Lord), for your light has come, and the glory of the Lord has risen upon you!

For behold, darkness shall cover the earth, and dense darkness [all] peoples, but the Lord shall arise upon you [O Jerusalem], and His glory shall be seen on you.

And nations shall come to your light, and kings to the brightness of your rising.

Isaiah said we can rise from the depression or the noise of the earth and come into the glory. Darkness covers the earth and the people, but His glory shall be seen on us—when we *rise* and *shine*. Then the nations will come to the light they see on us, even kings will come to the brightness of *your rising*…. But we must rise above. We must ascend and live from above.

The Release of Anointed Frequencies

New sounds are constantly being released from Heaven on the earth, and along with them an increase of angelic activity. There are dark sounds being released as well. That's why you have to watch what your children are listening to, because with each dark sound released on the earth, there is a demonic power released through it. If dark frequencies can release demonic power, then what kind of heavenly frequency does the new song release in the Church today? The new song releases anointed frequencies and angelic activity. The reason angels have not come forth in might and in power is they are not hearing the anointed sound in the churches. When that sound is there, you will see angelic activity like you've never seen before. Angels respond according to what they hear coming out of our mouths. What sound is on your voice?

When you're anointed, you have something on your voice that nobody else has unless they are anointed, too. This is documented.

The human voice is made up of atoms: there are atoms in your voice. If atoms are in your voice, then there's matter on your voice

If that is in the natural, what is it like when you get anointed? How much more matter do you have in your voice now that you are anointed? Dear friend, when you are anointed, there's enough matter in your voice to speak to the elements of nature.

Voice Print and Higher Frequency

Do you know that when God made man, He tuned man's body to His voice frequency? Every living thing is spinning with the vibration that comes from the voice of the Lord. Your body is spinning and has its form and is even now being sustained by the voice of His power. Hebrews 1:13 says:

> ...*He is the perfect imprint and very image of [God's] nature, upholding and maintaining and guiding and propelling the universe by* **His mighty word of power**... (Hebrews 1:3).

Sounds release either the demonic or the heavenly. This is how Jesus could walk through a wall. He carried a higher frequency than the wall. Do you know why you can cast out devils? You have a higher frequency. If you don't have a higher frequency, you can't cast it out.

Today, science calls this "voiceprint." Could voiceprint be the reason why demonic powers look at the Church and argue with it? Could it be because they know your voiceprint isn't real? "Jesus, I know Your voiceprint, but who are they?" We want to cast the devil out of someone or something, but cannot because the same demonic voiceprint resides in us. The demon says, "Your voiceprint corresponds with what's in me! You can't cast me out!"

We must be set free from the very thing we are trying to free others from or we will be powerless to get it done. In other words, how can you cast the spirit of addiction out of another individual if you have the same thing living in you? If you can't submit to the leadership in your life because you have a rebellious spirit, how can you expect your children to submit to you?

Do you remember Ella Fitzgerald, who could sing so high she could crack glass? If her natural ability could break matter, what do you really think that praise does in the Spirit? Your praise is supposed to break off principalities, it's supposed to break powers, and it's supposed to break up rulers of darkness. Your praise, your voiceprint, your praise level is a natural pulse that can break "glass."

Do you realize what you receive when you receive the Holy Spirit? I'm telling you, your voiceprint is dangerous to evil. Demon power knows your voiceprint. Angels know your voiceprint. And if you don't have the word of the Lord in your mouth, they won't respond to your words.

Sound also transmits visions, images, and color. When we talk, we often "see" what people are saying. You may have said to someone, "I see what you're saying." This means, if the people can't *see* what you are saying, they haven't heard it. "Faith comes by hearing" (Rom. 10:17) and by the Word of God. Faith comes by sound. It's important to hear and *see* what is being spoken.

Understanding God's Sound

You can learn what your gift for healing is when you start filling your life with worship frequencies. People ask me, "Jeff, why do miracles happen so easily in your meetings?" My response is, "Because of the revelation and release of God-sounds that bring the atmosphere for miracles to manifest."

The apostle Paul wrote:

Yet when we are among the full-grown (spiritually mature Christians who are ripe in understanding), we do impart a [higher] wisdom (the knowledge of the divine plan previously hidden); but it is indeed not a wisdom of this present age or of this world nor of the leaders and rulers of this age, who are being brought to nothing and are doomed to pass away.

But rather what we are setting forth is a wisdom of God once hidden [from the human understanding] and now revealed to us by God—[that wisdom] which God devised and decreed before the ages for our glorification [to lift us into the glory of His presence].

None of the rulers of this age or world perceived and recognized and understood this, for if they had, they would never have crucified the Lord of glory (1 Corinthians 2:6-8).

Revelation Brings Manifestation

Manifestations of the Spirit are coded. A person cannot walk in miracles, signs, and wonders without revelation. Revelation brings the manifestation. The manifestation confirms that the revelation comes from God. People cannot argue with the miracles. They may be able to argue with your doctrine, but they cannot fight miracles.

As Jesus taught, the power of the Lord was present with Him to heal.

One of those days, as He was teaching, there were Pharisees and teachers of the Law sitting by, who had come from every village and town of Galilee and Judea and from Jerusalem. And the power of the Lord was [present] with Him to heal them (Luke 5:17).

When revelation comes from Heaven, there is power for the manifestation. The devil hates revelation because it brings power with it for manifestation and healing. Hosea 4:6 says, *"My people are destroyed for lack of knowledge...."* Without revelation knowledge there is no empowerment.

Worldly Intellectualism

Intellectualism has become the means by which this present age determines reality. Worldly reasoning has become the meter by which humankind decides what is valid and real. This is humanistic at best. This kind of thinking is dangerous and antagonistic toward God. Worldly intellectualism is void of faith and power. Paul said:

> *by the power of signs and wonders, through the power of the Spirit of God. So from Jerusalem all the way around to Illyricum, I have fully proclaimed the gospel of Christ* (Romans 15:19 NIV).

> *My message and my preaching were not with wise and persuasive words, but with a demonstration of the Spirit's power...* (1 Corinthians 2:4-5).

Paul's preaching was done by the power of signs and wonders so that our faith might not rest in people but in the power of God. God wants to teach the Body of Christ how to access revelation knowledge from the heavens and manifest it on earth in substance. When Adam was created he had the mind of God, but when he fell, he traded the mind of God for an earthly mind based on human intellect and reason.

In the Garden of Eden, Adam didn't need faith because he already had everything he needed. Faith is required when you are in need. We require faith when things are closed off and we need to get them open again. The very first thing God gave Adam was faith so he could see the place from which he fell. It was the mercy of God for Adam to receive faith from God; otherwise he would have died from eternal grief. Adam needed to know that he would once again have access to the realm of glory from which he was created and from which he fell.

Time and matter became the basis of Adam's reality. This is why our intellect has a problem with anything that cannot be explained by our five senses. But the problem is, not all matter can be seen. Your intellect was never designed to distinguish between the visible and invisible realm. Paul said we look to the things that we cannot see. The unseen realm designed and created the realm that we detect with our five senses.

It is absolutely mandatory that we be transformed or renewed in our thinking in order to see the Kingdom of God. Jesus told Nicodemus:

*"I assure you, most solemnly I tell you, that unless a person is born again (anew, from above), he cannot ever **see** (know, be acquainted with, and experience) **the kingdom of God**"* (John 3:3).

We cannot "see" the Kingdom without first being born from above. We must undergo a complete spiritual metamorphosis of the Spirit in order to see in the Spirit. To undergo a transformation means to be formed back into the original state in which a thing was created. To be renewed is to bring something back to the original state or form when it was new. Paul said in Ephesians 4:23, *"be renewed in the spirit of your mind."*

Originally, we must have known both realms.

The natural mind can never show you a miracle. Common sense can never make a blind person see or a deaf person hear, nor reveal the reality of the glory realm, because common sense tells us that the natural realm is the boundary that defines what is real and what is not. This is antagonistic against God at best. This is antichrist or anti-anointing.

Revelation Unlocks Time, Space, and Matter

We have seen countless displays of creative miracles coming from Heaven by simply calling them into the natural when Heaven is open. When the glory of God is in the room, creative miracles are as easy as *"only speak a word, and my servant will be healed"* (Matt. 8:8 NKJV). When Heaven is open, you can see what is available there and pull it into time and space—and it will manifest.

I was in a meeting in South Korea a short time back with 6,000 people present. So many creative miracles took place that we couldn't keep track of them all. The meetings were televised and millions were watching all around Asia and the world. More were healed through television than those in the meetings, and the reports poured in. Out of all of the wonderful things God did, I remember on the last night of the meeting I called out that body parts were being recreated in the meeting. Along with the hundreds who came up to testify of miracles, there were several women who came up to testify that each had previously been missing a finger. In the glory, their missing fingers completely grew out and God even went as far as to put the right color fingernail polish on the nail to match the others!

When the heavens are open, all that we have need of is available and is as easy as calling it from the unseen realm into the visible by faith. I didn't think how the miracles were going to happen, I just saw it, spoke it, and it happened.

Revelation Knowledge

I don't think anyone really understands exactly what Adam experienced when he fell from the glory of God. When Adam fell, he traded the mind of Christ for the mind of reason. He went from experiential eating of the Tree of Life to eating from the tree of self-recognition and common sense. Common sense wants you to think and reason, but faith wants you to simply believe and react. This is why our intellect has problems with anything that cannot be explained. Not all matter is visible to the naked eye. Common sense bases reality on what is detected in the five natural senses, but this type of thinking or observation is incomplete.

God is Spirit. When God starts showing us what He wants to bring from the unseen realm of the glory, we need to start speaking it and manifesting the miracle in the natural. God is looking for a people who will move in revelation that will manifest Heaven on the earth, and He is working with people in this generation and this time to bring it about.

The society that we live in is largely educated to what we detect in our physical surrounding, and if we go beyond it we cannot conceive it. The only thing that can take you past your intellect is revelation knowledge. Jesus said in Mark 4:11:

> *To you has been entrusted the mystery of the kingdom of God [that is, the secret counsels of God which are hidden from the ungodly]; but for those outside [of our circle] everything becomes a parable.*

Revelation knowledge is the only thing that can bring us to the place of seeing the unseen realm. The natural mind and intellect can't do it. They are two completely different frequencies. The natural mind is incompatible with the mind of the Spirit. Common sense can't show you how to make a blind person see or a dead person live. Only revelation knowledge can show you these possibilities and realities. We need the mind of Christ.

Common sense says the physical realm is the boundary by which we are to define reality, and anything beyond that the mind cannot comprehend or believe. But a generation is rising that does not determine reality based upon what it can detect with the five senses, but rather determines reality based upon the Word of God and revelation knowledge.

The Spirit Realm and Resurrection Glory

The Book of Hebrews says that the things that we see with the natural eye were created by the things that we cannot see. They are made of unseen matter. The spirit realm holds matter together and maintains it. This applies to both the demonic realm as well as the supernatural Kingdom of God. Sickness is upheld by demonic tones or vibrations; the Father of lies speaks as well. If he can get us to agree with him and with his voice, he can bring sickness upon us. In order for that to happen, we must first agree to it. You see, we have the final say so on the outcome of our lives. By our words we are justified—and by our words we are condemned.

As the glory of God increases in the earth in the days to come, there will be a revival of the raising of the dead. When Jesus was raised from the grave on the third day, Scripture tells us that there was a mighty earthquake that shook the earth so violently that it opened up the graves, and many saints were seen walking through the streets of Jerusalem testifying the resurrection of the Lord Jesus Christ. There was such a glory released at the resurrection that those who had died in the Lord rose from their graves and were witnessed preaching in the streets. Now that's resurrection glory!

Death is nothing more than the spirit realm divorcing itself from the physical realm. The Spirit realm is the real realm that causes life to exist in the natural. When the spiritual breaks away from the natural, there is death. So, when the manifest presence of Almighty God is present in our atmosphere, that which is dead will be resurrected. When the true Spirit of God invades our atmosphere, all that is dead will get up. The raising of the dead will be the most common miracle done by common people in the coming glory revival.

Breaking Demonic Frequencies

I was in a meeting last year in New Zealand where the Spirit of the Lord moved powerfully with many creative miracles manifesting in the room. Testimony after testimony came forth of wonderful miracles and of instantaneous healings from the presence of the Lord. When the meeting was over, a man approached me from the back of the auditorium and said that he had brought his wife to the service. They had sat in the back during most of the meeting as she was not able to get up; her pain was so extreme. He proceeded to tell me that she had been suffering from stage four melanoma cancer and that the doctors gave her only two to four weeks to live. He asked me if I would pray for her and I agreed.

As the woman approached the front of the building, I could smell her before she came into focus. The stench of the spirit of cancer had engulfed her. She looked weak, weighing less than 100 pounds, and wearing a scarf as all of her hair had fallen out from the chemotherapy. Her husband helped to put her in the chair in the front row seat and then they turned their attention toward me.

As I began to walk toward her, I could feel the resistance from the spirit of cancer that was consuming her body. Yet, as I looked at her, something different happened. I said to the woman, "Honey, you don't have cancer! The doctors were wrong! You're going to be just fine." Without touching her, I turned around and walked away. I couldn't help but think that my actions appeared quite abrupt or even rude.

Several months later, the pastors from that church in Auckland, New Zealand, came to our 2010 Power and Glory of the Kingdom event in Murfreesboro, Tennessee. Immediately, Pastor Tim approached me and said, "Hey Jeff, great to see you! Do you remember the woman you prayed for at the end of the last event at our church last year?"

I had to think for a moment. "Yes, I remember the lady who came forward with her husband who was eaten up with cancer," I replied.

He said, "That's the one. I just wanted to let you know that all of her hair has grown back in and last week she went back to work at her old job. The doctors said she is a living miracle as all of the cancer in her body miraculously disappeared!"

Proverbs 18:21 says, *"Death and life are in the power of the tongue."*

What happened? This woman received a bad report from her doctor and then agreed with it, making it a powerful demonic decree. We need to be careful with what we agree. In Mark chapter 5, when Jairus received the report that his little girl was dead, Scripture states that Jesus overheard the report, but ignored it. He spoke to the heart and mind of Jairus and said, *"keep on believing"* (Mark 5:36). The power of agreement is key. We need to agree with the Word and the voice of the Spirit; and as we do, we will cancel out the voice of the enemy and break demonic agreements meant for our destruction.

The doctors may be right in diagnosing a situation and it may be a fact that you have a particular condition. But there is a higher truth available to us than plain fact. It's called *"by His stripes we are healed"* (Isaiah 53:5 NKJV). Truth in the Word trumps fact every time.

Matter and God-Sound Frequencies

According to science, sound and frequency are the exact same thing, but matter and frequency are different components and need each other to work. If you change the frequency in gold, the molecular structure will change and cause it to become a liquid. If you change the frequency of water, it will become a gas. In order to work in the miraculous, we need to understand we have authority to change and reclaim the natural through revelation declarations.

In Genesis, God said, *"Let there be,"* and the universe came from the sound of His voice. God called light from the unseen realm and the frequency of that light was His voice. He spoke, and it began to resonate and it became light: light, energy, matter, the universe, and then us—all from His voice. Everything we see in the natural came from God-sound frequencies.

If you develop a mole on your arm, that mole is merely a frequency that changed the molecular structure of your tissue from the original frequency. When we think of frequency, we automatically think of sound, but frequency goes far beyond what we hear with our ears.

What we set our eyes upon and allow into our mind is what will manifest in and around us. According to the law of focus, seeing produces thought, which in turn produces a light power that energizes seeds of desire. When these seeds reach maturity, they will bring forth according to their design.

What you focus on will chart the course of your present and future for good or bad. If you hold those thoughts until they are mixed with your emotions, desire releases the power of life and light and they birth. This principle is similar to what Jesus said:

Again I tell you, if two of you on earth agree (harmonize together, make a symphony together) about whatever [anything and everything] they may ask, it will come to pass and be done for them by My Father in heaven (Matthew 18:19).

This is the power of union and agreement. The power of agreement applies to God thoughts, fleshly desires, and demonic thoughts. Be careful with what you come into agreement.

According to scientific study and mentioned in David Van Koevering's audio message *The Science of God Sound,* when you *see* something, your brain responds with 700 times more firepower than when you hear a sound. This means that the eye gate is 700 times more powerful than the ear gate. If we limit God to hearing Him by sound alone, we are not hearing very much and are missing most of what He is saying.

Sin has a sound frequency as well and can bring you under the power of its voice. It will manifest around you as a dark light, which will pull an individual deeper into its power if not repented of by renouncing and changing the frequency.

The glory of God is the original pattern of which everything consists. The universe and the cosmos have their original set design from the voice of the Lord, but were drastically changed first by the fall of lucifer first, then the fall of man. God's cosmic realm, the glory realm, is still the original pattern for creation and will ultimately reframe and restore all that has been altered…but that's another book.

The Vibrating Voice of God

Given what we know from the Scriptures, it is not farfetched to imagine that God continuously sustains each unique vibration of all the various strings that constitute the building blocks of matter. Perhaps there is a different set of frequencies that are continuously released from the invisible realm of Heaven that sustain each individual note on every string simultaneously?

As we have already established, these are not ordinary sound waves like we are accustomed to on earth, because sound waves do not travel outside of earth's atmosphere. These are supernatural sounds that flow forth from the Spirit of God. While it is purely speculative, it is possible that there indeed is a "cosmic symphony" (to borrow terminology from Brian Greene's *The Elegant Universe*) of musical notes that continuously flow out of the throne of God in order to sustain the entire material universe. When this musical expression of the song of the Lord is ultimately withdrawn from creation, the elementary particles will literally melt with intense heat.

The Bible paints a glorious picture of the voice of God resounding over the whole creation. Not only did God speak the universe into existence with the power of His spoken Word, He also sustains the entire universe with the power of His voice. Both Ezekiel and the apostle John tell us that:

His voice was like the sound of many waters (Ezekiel 43:2; Revelation 1:15).

God's voice is not just a singular monotone; it is more like a tumultuous chorus of sounds and harmonies. Perhaps the voice of the Lord that sounds like *"many waters"* causes the frequencies of the many waters to resonate and shake.

*The voice of the Lord is upon the waters; the God of **glory thunders**; the Lord is upon many (great) waters. The voice of the Lord is **powerful**; the voice of the Lord is **full of majesty**. The voice of the Lord **breaks** the cedars; yes, the Lord breaks in pieces the cedars of Lebanon. … The voice of the Lord **splits and flashes forth forked lightning**. The voice of the Lord makes the **wilderness tremble**; the Lord **shakes** the Wilderness of Kadesh. The voice of the Lord makes the hinds bring forth their young, and His voice **strips bare the forests**, while in His temple everyone is saying, Glory!* (Psalm 29:3-9).

The Bible reveals that Jesus Christ is the Lord of all creation and that all creation *trembles* at His mighty voice. His voice *shakes* or *vibrates* the very fabric of the earth at a sub-atomic level. The Hebrew word for "shake" is *chuwl* and it means to dance or to tremble. God makes the quantum world to *dance* and *tremble* at the sound of His voice.

He shakes the earth from its place and makes its pillars tremble (Job 9:6 NIV).

God not only shakes the earth, He also shakes the heavens.

*Therefore I will make the heavens **tremble**, and the earth will be **shaken** from its place…* (Isaiah 13:13 NASB).

*The Lord's voice will **roar** from Zion and **thunder** from Jerusalem, and **the earth and heavens will** to **shake**…* (Joel 3:16 NLT).

*The pillars of **heaven tremble** and are astonished at His rebuke* (Job 26:11).

God's voice resonates over all creation and all creation has been skillfully designed to respond to the resonance of the voice of Him who sounds like *"many waters."* I think it is significant that He whose voice sounds like many waters is revealed as being upon the many waters. Perhaps this is an ancient and pre-scientific way of saying that the harmonics and higher and lower octaves of His glorious voice actually vibrate the many waters at a quantum level.

God Knew You Before Time

There was never a time that you were not in the mind of God. From the beginning, before your birth, He knew you. Before you had a dirt body and the atomic structure that forms your shape, God knew you and was singing your song frequency. We are eternal, and birthed by an eternal God, given a destiny and a holy calling to be fulfilled from before the foundation of the world:

> [For it is He] Who delivered and saved us and called us with a calling in itself holy and leading to holiness [to a life of consecration, a vocation of holiness]; [He did it] not because of anything of merit that we have done, but because of and to further His own purpose and grace (unmerited favor) which was given us in Christ Jesus before the world began [eternal ages ago] (2 Timothy 1:9).

Before the worlds were framed and placed into their cosmic order, we existed and were given a holy calling and destiny to be fulfilled for this planet. Not only that, but we were completely known by Him. We are not some invaluable thing abortion can snuff the life frequency out of. God knew our framework before placing each of us in our mother's womb. He has a destiny, a purpose, and a plan for us, though many miss it.

If we have faith, we can see what God sees using spiritual perception to know what He knows. It is in this place that you can see yourself in a different light, and that revelation will change your world.

For as he thinks in his heart, so is he (Proverbs 23:7).

As you see what God observes, your framework will change, calling the nonexistent things as though they already are. It's all about frequency.

The Harmonious Frequency of the Glory Realm

How full of the Spirit are you? Do you have capacity enough to see your future? This isn't New Age, it's *Kingdom Age*. By the anointing, you know all things.

But you have been anointed by [you hold a sacred appointment from, you have been given an unction from] the Holy One, and you all know [the Truth] or you know all things (1 John 2:20).

When the Fall took place, the molecular structure of creation changed in an instant of time and humans lost the ability to know their destiny as heavenly citizens. But you have a memory, you can remember yesterday, and you have an anointing from the Holy One. By faith you can be lifted up to see the place from which you fell—from the realm of glory.

For all have sinned and fall short of the Glory of God (Romans 3:23 NKJV).

The Book of Romans clearly states that when Adam fell in the Garden, he fell from a place. That place was called the glory of God. We can be restored to the glory of God by faith in Jesus Christ. Jesus said that when the Holy Spirit comes, you will know all things—you will know all truth. He will only speak the things He has heard from the Father, and He will show you things to come. They are printed on your spirit, and you will see what God sees and know your destiny.

The glory realm is here, but many are not tuned in to it because they are too much in their own mind and not the mind of Christ. We need to let God speak His voice, His science, His frequency, His sound into us—and we will be complete.

He made you a certain way. Find out what God has created you to become and resonate there. Don't try to be something you are not. Find out what it is that He designed you to be, and you will flourish.

CHAPTER 12

MENTAL *METAMORPHOO*

The mind is the battlefield in spiritual warfare. Satan is very much aware of this and constantly assaults our minds, his greatest battlefields. Whoever wins the battle for our minds is whose servants we become. Paul commanded us to think on virtuous things (see Phil. 4:8). We cannot allow our minds to dwell upon evil or things that are incompatible with God and expect to be compatible with Him.

> *Do not be deceived: "Evil company corrupts good habits"* (1 Corinthians 15:33 NKJV).

We have within us the ability to renew our minds and be transformed. The mind is malleable. Humans have a creative capacity. We operate in that capacity either consciously or unconsciously. Thoughts are seeds. When thoughts are connected with strong emotion, conception takes place. If that seed is nurtured and incubated, it will reproduce according to the pattern of thought through which it was conceived, whether evil or good. Seed thoughts will manifest and come to pass. One of the most important laws of creation is that all things reproduce after their own likeness and kind. Your thoughts, too, will reproduce after their own kind.

Reprogramming the Mind

The human mind is difficult to understand. The human brain is an incredible bioelectric, magnetic mass of grey matter, and works similar to a computer. We use our brains to think, to analyze and disseminate information, and to arrive at conclusions. Although a computer cannot originate thought, it is programmable. The mind is programmable, too. It can be programmed with ideas, concepts, knowledge, and values, and will run according to its programming.

Satan wants to program your mind to run according to his program, with lies and values that are contrary to God's thoughts and ways. Just watch some television for a while and see how many anti-God concepts vie for space in your mind.

There's a very real all-out assault for your mind out there. The greatest battlefield in the threefold nature of humans (body, soul, and spirit) is the mind, not the spirit. Satan knows that if he can capture your mind, your thinking will be off kilter and then the whole person will be off.

When your mind is healthy, your eye will be healthy, and your whole body will be full of light. When your mind is free and clean, the doorway is open for God's love and light to flow in and through you. We all need to get our thought lives aligned with the purposes and Word of God and understand the way He thinks. The good news is that God sent us an instruction manual that explains the marvel of the mind and how to use it. The book is the Bible, and it reveals valuable keys to the right and proper use of the mind. It explains why we're incapable, in and of ourselves, to work out His purpose without His divine intervention.

Metamorphosis—the Necessity of Transformation

The Greek word *metamorphoo* is translated into the English word "transformed" as found in Romans 12:2. As stated earlier, the word *metamorphoo* means metamorphosis, which is the process a caterpillar goes through in the cocoon. It enters as a worm and leaves as a beautiful butterfly.

And do not be conformed to this world, but be transformed by the renewing of your mind, so that you may prove what the will of God is, that which is good and acceptable and perfect (Romans 12:2 NASB).

A caterpillar crawls along the ground and conforms to all of the earth's contours. A butterfly, on the other hand, soars above the earth. Paul is exhorting the believers in Rome not to conform to the world with its traditions and ways of thinking. He is saying that our entire lives will be transformed and metamorphosed when our minds are renewed. This will allow us to soar and not have to conform to the world's standards of living and being; fully capable of proving the good and acceptable and perfect will of God.

A *mindset* is when our minds are programmed and set to respond a specific way or project a certain impression when encountering different words, pictures, situations, etc. For example, when the word "church" is stated, many have a very definite impression about the topic. They have preconceived thoughts and feelings about church because of previous experiences that have been grafted into their minds: a church they attended when they were younger, a religious fanatic they watched on television, or the enthusiastic preacher on the car radio, for a few examples.

For most of us, our mindsets are in the caterpillar state—the worm that is still conformed to this world. That mindset, however, is about to be changed and renewed. The bride of Christ is about to become a very heavenly creature. Many people will look for her crawling along the ground but will miss her as she soars overhead.

Ungodly and worldly mindsets are spiritual strongholds that restrain us from soaring. These bondages are broken by the transformation that comes from the pressure and isolation in the cocoon. The Greek word *thlipsis* is translated into the English word tribulation, which literally means pressure.

We are liberated through the constrictions and pressures that the Lord allows to come upon us in the cocoon. The restraints of self-dependence are broken as we rely more and more on the Spirit of God—being strengthened in our inner self so we can rise to higher altitudes. Those who want to avoid these trials will be confined as worms to the earth. We can choose to move with the current of the Spirit and let the trials of this present age work for us, or we can continue to wade through the shallow water and never reach our destination, which only comes after the rapids. Jesus says:

> *Whoever finds his [lower] life will lose it [the higher life], and whoever loses his [lower] life on My account will find it [the higher life]* (Matthew 10:39).

Paul says in Romans 8:18:

> *[But what of that?] For I consider that the sufferings of this present time (this present life) are not worth being compared with the glory that is about to be revealed to us and in us and for us and conferred on us!*

Unfortunately, many leaders, from a lack of maturity, have kept the church in a state of infancy. They are in danger of losing all.

This metamorphosis is mandatory. Trying to save someone from it is doing the person harm. The chick needs the struggle of getting out of the egg to produce blood flow into its extremities. If not, there's a good chance of losing its life after birth. The struggle for life is necessary for walking in the fullness of life.

Mental Receptors and Gateways

When thoughts and emotions blend, there starts a creative process of birthing in the thought life and in the realm of the imagination. Satan knows this, so he wants your mind. The mind is a receptor and open to spiritual influences both light and dark. Jesus talks about dark light in Matthew 6:23:

> *But if your eye is unsound, your whole body will be full of dark-ness. If then the very light in you [your conscience] is darkened, how dense is that darkness!*

Dark light is the belief that something is true when in actuality it is a deception. The inference is to be careful of the thing you believe to be light, when indeed it is dark. Why? The mind is the gateway and connector to all incoming spiritual communication.

The mind is a part of the physical body. The brain is a physical organ and is different from the mind. The brain is the physical housing and connector used by the mind to translate spiritually inspired information communicated from the realm of the spirit. The brain then transfers this information into the natural. Bill Johnson states in his audio teaching, *The Supernatural Power of the Renewed Mind:*

> God didn't design the mind to be an originator of thought. Rather, He designed the mind to act as an internal processor

capable of receiving programmable information—information that could be programmed into the "system."

Whoever programs your mind will determine the way you think and what your life will become—your destiny. Within your mind is the foundation of what you really believe about what you say you believe and the associated emotions that stem from and reinforce the choices you make. Satan will try to win the right to your mind so that he can program it just the way he wants.

However, God created people's spirits with the ability to receive inspired supernatural information directly from Him, with the capacity to direct and influence the mind, will, emotions, and flesh to manifest in the natural what we receive from Him in the spirit. Consider that God is Spirit, and He created us with the very breath of His Spirit. Humans, as spirits, do have the capacity to create and originate thought. This is the wonderful and powerful dimension from which all miracles, signs, and wonders come from that manifest out of the realm of glory.

Human Intellect

On earth, humans are the only created beings that possess a spirit, intellect, and reason. We also have thoughts, emotions, and behaviors unique to us as spirit beings created in the image of God. Humans are capable of loving God; the inferior creatures are not. This is the specific difference between humans and animals.

The animal kingdom relies on instinct, inborn behaviors not on experience. How does a salmon know to swim to where it was born to lay its eggs and die? How do birds know how far south to fly? How do homing pigeons find their way home? We can originate thought, but animals cannot. Everything animals know has been preprogrammed or may be programmed into them.

We, on the other hand, don't instinctively know everything we need to know. The psalmist wrote: *"I am fearfully and wonderfully made"* (Ps. 139:14 NKJV). This is true of your brain—it is amazing—but it is also incomplete in that we must constantly acquire physical and spiritual knowledge.

Acquiring Knowledge

We gain physical knowledge with our five senses. We see, hear, smell, touch, and taste, and constantly add to our knowledge base. Similarly, we gain spiritual knowledge by developing and using our spiritual senses. When we draw close to God and allow God to strengthen, teach, and lead us through and by His Spirit, spiritual desires spring forth and we accomplish spiritual things. With a Spirit-led mind, we will find the way into that supernatural realm of God's Kingdom to find all of its treasures. If we can spiritually see God's Kingdom, we will desire it all the more.

The human spirit was designed by God to receive knowledge and understanding. Using this revelation, we decipher information from the physical world with our five senses, and are then able to see, touch, smell, hear, and taste things from the spiritual realm by God's Spirit.

Each of us has the privilege and awesome responsibility of programming our own brain "run" according to this programming. Sometimes we end up with wrong programming that runs contrary to the design of God. However, when we are born again, we are supernaturally infused with the holy seed of God. In that very seed is *all* of who God is. In time, with the proper care from the Holy Spirit and the Word, that seed will grow and bear the exact likeness and makeup of the original seed. Contained in the seed is all that God is spiritually, and the very likeness and image of Christ Jesus.

Reprogramming Your Mind

The transformation process begins when there is a harmony between your mind and your spirit. Harmony comes through freedom from blockages in the mind. If your mind runs against the truth, the seed in your spirit cannot grow, or else it grows and produces the wrong fruit. Cast out everything that is not the truth of God's Word, and the truth will renew your mind and bring forth rapid growth in your life. Quickened-truth is when revelation comes and you receive it. Revelation carries with it the power to renew your mind.

> *For who has known or understood the mind (the counsels and purposes) of the Lord so as to guide and instruct Him and give Him knowledge?...* (1 Corinthians 2:16).

Your mind is the gateway between the spirit and physical realm of the whole person, so your mind and spirit must agree. When you were born again, your spirit and mind were not compatible. Therefore, it's an ongoing process to reprogram the mind to conform to the mind of Christ in your spirit. Deposited in your spirit is the mind of Christ. Yes, your spirit has a mind—the very mind of Christ. Consider Ephesians 4:23: *"and be constantly renewed in the spirit of your mind [having a fresh mental and spiritual attitude]."*

Your spirit can originate thought on its own, but it can also be inspired to originate thought. This occurs when the brain and the spirit are compatible. They must be in harmony or there will be blockages. The brain will sift and sort information it receives; but unless it is in harmony with the spirit, the spirit will not receive and be filled with light.

But the natural, nonspiritual man does not accept or welcome or admit into his heart the gifts and teachings and revelations of the Spirit of God, for they are folly (meaningless nonsense) to him; and he is incapable of knowing them (of progressively recognizing, understanding, and becoming better acquainted with them) because they are spiritually discerned and estimated and appreciated (1 Corinthians 2:14).

The natural mind is the mind or the soul-life programmed with the concepts of this world and the kingdom of darkness. The spiritual believer must be programmed with different thinking.

Now we have not received the spirit [that belongs to] the world, but the [Holy] Spirit Who is from God, [given to us] that we might realize and comprehend and appreciate the gifts [of divine favor and blessing so freely and lavishly] bestowed on us by God (1 Corinthians 2:12).

But the person who is united to the Lord becomes one spirit with Him (1 Corinthians 6:17).

The First Step to the Renewed Mind

Your spirit has become one with the Lord. Everything that is God is already in your spirit. We are joined to the Lord and are *"one spirit with Him."* We must align the brain with the spirit, bringing them both into unity so they are not running on separate programs.

Do not be conformed to this world (this age), [fashioned after and adapted to its external, superficial customs], but be transformed (changed) by the [entire] renewal of your mind [by its new ideals and its new attitude], so that you may prove [for

*yourselves] what is the good and acceptable and perfect will of
God, even the thing which is good and acceptable and perfect
[in His sight for you]* (Romans 12:2).

Your brain has to be transformed from the soulish concepts of
the world by the Word of God and renewed, whether understood
or not. There are many things in the Word of God that we have
yet to understand. We read things and pass them by because there
is a layer there that is not coming through to us. However, God's
Word is truth whether we understand it or not. And, the first step
starts with *accepting God's Word whether we understand it or not.*
It is God's Word and accepting it is the first step in renewal. The
greatest hindrance to walking with God is the unrenewed brain.

*Finally, brothers and sisters, whatever is true, whatever is
noble, whatever is right, whatever is pure, whatever is lovely,
whatever is admirable—if anything is excellent or praisewor-
thy—think about such things* (Philippians 4:8).

This Scripture should remind us to guard our minds at all
times. It should act as a filter that we place over our minds. If it is
not true, honest, or pure—reject it. God has placed this warning in
the Bible to keep our minds clean and running right, and flowing
with the light and love of God. The apostle Paul, in his letter to the
Romans, recorded an amazing statement:

*[That is] because the mind of the flesh [with its carnal thoughts
and purposes] is hostile to God, for it does not submit itself to
God's Law; indeed it cannot* (Romans 8:7).

In other words, the natural mind is an enemy of God. This
statement provides startling insight into the workings of the

carnal, natural mind. Cut off from God, the mind is an enemy of God—the mind hates Him. Your spirit may be born again, but if your mind is unrenewed there is conflict. Your spirit flows through the mind, and truth is blocked or corrupted and altered because of wrong concepts.

If we can get our spirits compatible with the way our brains think, there will be a unity that opens a supernatural gateway from Heaven, allowing transforming light, understanding, and knowledge to flow into our beings. Then we will understand the mysteries of creation and the universe. We will understand God and the purposes of God, because our brains will be in harmony with Him. The supernatural pathways only open when the two become compatible.

You Are an Ancient Spirit

Your spirit came from Heaven and has been in existence for a long time. I am talking spirit here; not soul. The soul can die. God can take the soul, or the soul can be forfeited by a person. The soul can also be saved and redeemed (see Ps. 116:4; 2 Sam. 4:9; Ps. 86:13). Therefore, the soul is what each person is as a human being. A person cannot exist outside of the soul. The Old Testament reveals nothing about any preexistence or immortality of the soul.

But the spirit is another matter. It preexisted in Heaven. However, it is clothed in the soul. Your spirit came into your body at birth. It was God's intention that we grow beyond just spirit and become a new creation. That's why Paul prayed:

> *...and may your spirit and soul and body be preserved sound and complete [and found] blameless at the coming of our Lord Jesus Christ (the Messiah)* (1 Thessalonians 5:23).

It is important that we—as spirit, soul, and body—blend as one. Heaven was first a spiritual world. But God created the earth and brought Heaven into it, into a physical dimension. When you were born again, Christ came into your spirit. That seed is more than just spirit. You are a living soul and the mind is the key.

The Book of Romans tells us that to be spiritually minded is life and peace, but to be carnally minded is death. The natural mind has programming from another kingdom—the kingdom of darkness.

The battle is on for programming rights to your mind!

Whoever gets the rights to program your mind, gets you. Yes, the Holy Spirit can and does erase wrong programming. However, keeping it programmed correctly is vital. If you do not keep your mind rightly programmed, you will fall back into the mess out of which you came.

Demons or evil spirits can influence the pathways of thinking and corrupt the imagination. When this happens, it filters any pure light of revelation coming to us, leading to a need for deliverance. The demonic spirit can attach itself to our thought lives and imagination; and if allowed, it will create a spiritual stronghold.

Evil spirits can build strongholds and attach themselves to us as a false way of thinking. As our mind is being renewed, they cannot hold on any longer and the doors or pathways close. The more the mind is renewed, the more we starve the evil spirits, and eventually they give up. We have to be diligent door-closers because the spirits have an incredible capacity to interact with the mind; projecting pictures, thoughts, and concepts. If we do not object, they can nest in our minds and even multiply.

The Most Excellent Way

Humankind, like God, has a creative ability that can be exercised through the mind to recreate the world around us. Again, Psalm 139:14 says that we *"are fearfully and wonderfully made."*

We were created in the image and likeness of God. The same creative nature of God is resident within us. Creative authority is best released through love, which is the most excellent way. With all that has been given to humanity, in terms of the gifts of the Holy Spirit and the ability to cooperate with the Spirit of God in the anointing, there still remains a fuller and more abundant way to minister the mind, heart, and power of God in the earth. Paul says:

> *But earnestly desire and zealously cultivate the greatest and best gifts and graces (the higher gifts and the choicest graces). And yet I will show you a still **more excellent way** [one that is better by far and the highest of them all—**love*** (1 Corinthians 12:31).

What is the more excellent way? Love.

> *For we know in part and we prophesy in part; but when the perfect comes, the partial will be done away. When I was a child, I used to speak like a child, think like a child, and reason like a child; when I became a man, I did away with childish things. For now we see in a mirror dimly, but then face to face; now I know in part, but then I will know fully just as I also have been fully known. But now faith, hope, love, abide these three; but **the greatest of these is love*** (1 Corinthians 13:9-13 NKJV).

Many people take the phrase, *"when the perfect comes,"* and conclude it is referring to the second coming of Christ. The phrase, however, is talking about love. The entire 13th chapter of First

Corinthians talks about love and our lives being perfected in love. Paul wrote about a new standard, a new level. He says we should earnestly desire the best gifts and graces, but there is still a better way—the way of love. What are the childish things Paul refers to? They are "in part" and "partial." The childish things we are called to put away are *knowing in part* and *understanding in part*—so we can *entirely* and *fully* know Him who is love.

This glory move of God will be carried out with the stamp of Galatians 5:6 (NKJV), "...*but faith working through love.*"

Without this quality of love, we will never be connected with the heart of God in this most excellent way. When that which is perfect has come, looking through a glass darkly will be done away with. We will come to this perfection of love—from one level to another—more fully, deeply, and intimately.

Thoughts Birthed from Passion

It's important to keep in mind that thoughts are seeds; thoughts contain life and will reproduce. As mentioned earlier, the "Creation Law of Reproduction" simply means all things reproduce after their own kind. Genesis 1:11-12 says:

> *And God said, Let the earth put forth [tender] vegetation: plants yielding seed and fruit trees yielding fruit whose seed is in itself, each according to its kind, upon the earth. And it was so. The earth brought forth vegetation: plants yielding seed according to their own kinds and trees bearing fruit in which was their seed, each according to its kind. And God saw that it was good (suitable, admirable) and He approved it.*

This creation law affects us continually as it shapes our future and determines our present. Even now our circumstances are being determined by this law. We need to stop blaming everybody else, including the devil, for our present circumstances and take responsibility for what is growing in our lives. This creation law is irrevocable and unchangeable. We plant trees and gardens and they reproduce after their kind. The fertile soil where we unknowingly plant most seeds that spring up is in the garden of our hearts.

What you plant there *will* reproduce and come forth. Thoughts *are* seeds. Passion and strong desire are the heat that causes the seed to spin into life. Babies are conceived in passion. So too, inner passion gives life to the seeds in your heart.

For as he thinks in his heart, so is he (Proverbs 23:7).

This means that what we believe and think in our hearts, so we will become. What we think about will be manifested in our lives. In Matthew 7:1-2, Jesus says that if you judge, you will be judged; and in the same measure you judge with, you will be judged also. The seed of judgment sown will reap a tree of judgment. Because of this law, we must live every moment, in thought and action, as we desire the future to be. The human mind is one of the greatest earthly powers. This is what Jesus has in mind when He says:

> *Truly I say to you, whoever says to this mountain, "Be taken up and cast into the sea," and does not doubt in his heart, but believes that what he says is going to happen, it will be done for him* (Mark 11:23).

Jesus isn't speaking metaphorically, He's talking literally. You don't even have to be a Christian for this to work. There are many people displaying supernatural feats and abilities illegally by this principle alone. Remember, the human mind is a great earthly power—this universal law cannot be changed. Jesus goes on to further explain this truth in verse 24:

For this reason I am telling you, whatever you ask for in prayer, believe (trust and be confident) that it is granted to you, and you will [get it] (Mark 11:24).

Jesus is saying to believe, to be confident and desire what you are asking for, and you will receive it. Our thoughts aren't momentary insignificant blurbs, but are the seeds of desire that produce and chart the course of our present and future life.

If thoughts are seeds, then how are they planted? When a thought firmly connects with an emotion, a supernatural power is released and the seed begins to grow. If both the emotion and thought are positive, the seed brings forth light and life. This principle is similar to:

If two of you agree on earth concerning anything…it will be done for them (Matthew 18:19 NKJV).

When your emotions agree with your thinking, it shall be done. This is the power of union and agreement. It works for both God thoughts and demonic thoughts. Love, for example, is when your spouse comes home from work and gives you a big kiss and tells you with warm affection you are loved. When the connection takes place between your thoughts and your emotions, it begins to fill your entire being and becomes a living force. This seed of thought, when energized by emotion, will literally create an environment of love and joy around your entire household, and it will be felt.

Any thoughts that connect with our emotions become a very strong power and determine the atmosphere around us. The church has taught for years that emotions are not important. I say to you that emotions, as well as your thought life, are the creative side of you. Your emotions are essential for everything to happen. Jesus was moved with the emotion of compassion and released miracles:

And Jesus, in pity, touched their eyes; and instantly they received their sight and followed Him (Matthew 20:34).

Compassion releases miracles…even the raising of the dead:

Soon afterward, Jesus went to a town called Nain, and His disciples and a great throng accompanied Him. [Just] as He drew near the gate of the town, behold, a man who had died was being carried out—the only son of his mother, and she was a widow; and a large gathering from the town was accompanying her. And when the Lord saw her, He had compassion on her and said to her, Do not weep. And He went forward and touched the funeral bier, and the pallbearers stood still. And He said, Young man, I say to you, arise from death]! And the man [who was] dead sat up and began to speak. And [Jesus] gave him [back] to his mother (Luke 7:11-15).

The power and glory of God in the anointing are released through the gateway of human affection. It's important that we are connected with our emotions and not shut down. We can be limited by our lack of compassion. This is why Paul said to the Corinthian church, "*…you are restricted by your own affections*" (2 Corinthians 6:12 NKJV).

We have to feel what we do. When our thinking connects with our feelings, a seed is planted by desire and a power is released. James says: "*when desire has conceived, it gives birth to sin; and sin, when it is full-grown, brings forth death*" (James 1:15 NKJV).

Thoughts Are a Spiritual Offering

We need to be careful what we are thinking. Every time we think, we place a spiritual offering at the door that energizes and powers that thought. An evil desire is conceived when the thought and the emotion come together. This forms a creative power bond of agreement that "brings forth" death. "Brings forth" means to *breed or create*, and is the same as a plant that is produced from the seed. It is the Creation Law of Reproduction at work.

When I meditate on the Word and revelation begins to flow, my whole being seems to be flooded with light—not only light, but flooded with the tranquil peace and life of God. The revelation that comes from God's mind flows through my emotions and makes a place in my spirit for seeds to be planted and grow. Remember, revelation isn't just an abstract thought, it is connected with a feeling that buries life deep inside us. When seeds are planted, conception has taken place. If watered, the revelation will give birth in our lives. As we think, so we will become.

Taking Back the Creative Power of Imagination

As I briefly mentioned earlier, there are keys we need to employ to unlock the realm of glory such as vision, imagination, and faith. This new glory generation will move in the understanding of how to release wonders in the creative power of the imagination. They will birth the will and purposes of God on the earth with mind-blowing authority over physical elements in the natural realm.

The creative power of the imagination is not a New Age or occult principle: it is a Kingdom reality created by God to manifest in the natural what is seen in the spirit. The demonic world of the occult can use it to birth destruction in the natural by curses that materialize from unholy allegiances. But God gave us an imagination to come under the influence of the Holy Spirit and birth life, freedom, and destiny into our lives.

Unfortunately, we've been taught to believe that using our imagination in conjunction with our spirit is New Age and used to advance the kingdom of darkness. In reality, New Agers and occultists stole something very precious from the saints of God and have perverted it to the point that we are afraid to come near it. It's time to take back the power to envision. It's time we start using what God gave to us to wreak havoc on the kingdom of darkness.

We must visualize what we desire to become in God. Actually, we must see ourselves as we really are in Christ, then it will manifest as reality in our lives. The imagination is a creative tool that brings into the physical world that which sits dormant in the unseen realm. We can use our imagination to transform the world around us; both for good and for evil.

Look to Heaven and Visualize

You cannot walk in something until you see yourself walking in it. You may say, "Visualizing is New Age." But the truth is, you've been visualizing since you were born. Every time you think about something, every time you daydream, you're visualizing.

It's part of the thinking process. It's easy to blame the devil and others for things that happen to us in life, but in actuality, our present circumstances are the direct result of where our heart is set in thought. We are reaping the harvest of what we have thought, envisioned, and sowed. Jesus considered the imagination as reality. He says in Matthew 5:28 (NASB):

"Everyone who looks at a woman with lust for her has already committed adultery with her in his heart."

When we look with our eyes and think wrongly in our minds, we have committed and birthed the act of adultery in our heart— it's already done. The mind and the imagination are the same thing. It's just as if you had already done it.

Abraham Imagined

When Abraham was an old man, God promised that his descendants would be like the stars. How was it possible for Abraham to become the father of two great nations? God told him to look into Heaven, to look at the stars. Abraham set his eyes to the heavens and looked: he imagined. He believed. This impossible situation became possible when Abraham visualized it as a reality. As he looked at the stars, he saw his family.

God wants us to be active in our part of stepping into our destinies. God speaks the promise, but we fail to look up, we fail to visualize, we fail to see the impossible situation with eyes of faith. When we use our imaginations according to the promises of God, the impossible becomes possible.

In his book *Fourth Dimension*, Dr. Paul Yonggi Cho (David Cho) explains how the Holy Spirit incubated the earth when it was without form and substance as a physical planet. God also expects us to be active in the incubation of our faith by visualizing the final results of His promise. Dr. Cho says:

My church has not grown to its present membership of 275,000 people because I am the most gifted pastor in the world. No. It has grown to its present size because I have followed Abraham's principle of visualization. In 1984, I see my church having half a million members. I can count them. I can see their faces in my heart.

As of 2007, Dr. Cho's church had 830,000 members and by 2014 the number increased to 1 million. I think he's onto something.

God calls those things that are not as though they already exist. When the earth was formless and void, God already saw it with form and substance and simply called it forth. Our words must agree with our vision in order to bring them to pass. Paul said:

Yet we have the same spirit of faith as he had who wrote, I have believed, and therefore have I spoken. We too believe, and therefore we speak (2 Corinthians 4:13).

If we see ourselves sick, broken down, and impoverished, that is exactly what will be birthed in our lives. If we begin to imagine ourselves as blessed of God and start calling those things that are not as though they are, they will manifest in our lives. Regardless of our race, gender, financial condition, or family situation, we must believe and speak. As Abraham looked up at the stars and imagined his God-promised family, let us look at Heaven and believe and speak His promises to us.

Let It Be Done the Way You Imagine

And when Jesus entered Capernaum, a centurion came to Him, imploring Him, and saying, "Lord, my servant is lying paralyzed at home, fearfully tormented." Jesus said to him, "I will come and heal him." But the centurion said, "Lord, I am not worthy for You to come under my roof, but just say the word, and my servant will be healed. For I also am a man under authority, with soldiers under me; and I say to this one, 'Go!' and he goes, and to another, 'Come!' and he comes, and to my slave, 'Do this!' and he does it." Now when Jesus heard this, He marveled and said to those who were following, "Truly I say

to you, I have not found such great faith with anyone in Israel.
And Jesus said to the centurion, "Go; it shall be done for you as
you have believed." And the servant was healed that moment
(Matthew 8:5-10,13 NASB).

From this passage of Scripture in Matthew 8, we can pull several significant teachings on the topics of faith, believing, and healing, among many others. But the solitary lesson I want to draw from this passage is that of faith in relationship to our imagination. I believe our imaginations are part of our creative nature. Everything God spoke into existence already existed in His mind and in His heart. Everything that a person builds first lives within—within his or her imagination.

Trust Is a Matter of the Heart

We know that faith is not just a matter of the mind, but of the heart. When God asks us to have faith in Him, He is asking us to trust Him. Trust is a matter of the heart. But true faith doesn't just stay in the heart. Indeed, faith first springs from the heart, but eventually floods the rest of the individual, including the mind, imagination, and, in time, every action and word.

In the story of the faith of the centurion, we see Jesus saying that He would go to the centurion's servant to heal him. Jesus was perfectly fine with going the distance, but the centurion believed within himself that his servant would be healed if only Jesus spoke the word. Because he was a man of authority, a man of the spoken word, he had his mind made up and was firmly convinced in the authority of the spoken word. His faith was in the spoken word. Read Jesus' response: *"Go your way; and as you have believed, let it be done for you"* (Matt. 8:13 NKJV).

It's in the way you believe, the way you imagine, and where your faith rests. For example, many people believe God is more likely to heal them of cancer in a Benny Hinn meeting than at a local church meeting. If that's where your faith rests, by all means, get to that meeting. But if you are firmly convinced in your mind and heart that God can heal you through watching Benny Hinn on television, then you will be healed as you watch him in your living room. But if your faith rests in the healing word of God, I'm sure you'll daily claim Isaiah 53:5 over yourself: "By His stripes I am healed." Because imagination helps cultivate faith and belief, you can say, "As I imagine, it will be done unto me."

Dianoia and *Photizo*

[For I always pray to] the God of our Lord Jesus Christ, the Father of glory, that He may grant you a spirit of wisdom and revelation [of insight into mysteries and secrets] in the [deep and intimate] knowledge of Him, by having the eyes of your heart flooded with light, so that you can know understand the hope to which He has called you, and how rich is His glorious inheritance in the saints (His set-apart ones) (Ephesians 1:17-18).

The Greek word for "understanding" in the verse above is *dianoia*, which properly means "to exercise your mind or imagination."

Also, "flooded with light," in other Bible translations is the word "enlighten," which is the Greek word *photizo*, which means "to brighten or illuminate," as in taking a picture. It's where we get our word "photograph." The passage in Ephesians 1 says that the eyes of your understanding will be enlightened and illuminated as you exercise and engage your imagination.

Paul said we walk by faith: *"for we walk by faith…not by sight or appearance"* (2 Cor. 5:7). Real faith is seeing the unseen. Paul said that we walk, not by natural sight, but by seeing in the spirit.

Since we consider and look not to the things that are seen but to the things that are unseen; for the things that are visible are temporal (brief and fleeting), but the things that are invisible are deathless everlasting (2 Corinthians 4:18).

When we look with the eyes of our heart, with the eyes of our imagination, we are gazing into the eternal realm.

Imagination Creates Your World

Webster's New World Dictionary defines the word "imagine" as "to make a mental image, to conceive in the mind, and to suppose and think." This is saying that we conceive and come up with ideas in the mind, which have no *tangible* or *touchable* foundation. It defines the word "imagination" as "the act or power of forming mental images of what is not present, and the act or power of creating new ideas." The imagination is our gift from God that should be used as a tool to create and manifest the unseen into the visible realm.

God created us to be thinking, imaginative, and visionary people who, with the sanctified imagination, like God calls into being that which does not exist (see Rom. 4:17).

God gave us the power to create. We are inventive and creative like our Father in Heaven. Every physical item that surrounds you right now, whether it's a clock, a picture frame, or a coffee cup, has a certain amount of imagination and creative design put into it. Every masterpiece ever created first existed in the imagination of the artist.

Engaging in Revelation

If we're hungry about moving in the same kinds of experiences Ezekiel or Isaiah had, we need to start meditating over their third heaven experiences and start asking the Lord for our own. We need to take time to soak in the powerful presence of the Holy Spirit and use our imagination to engage Heaven.

When we engage ourselves in this manner, it's only a matter of time before we find ourselves before the very throne of God. God is the rewarder of those who passionately seek Him. God loves dreamers and visionaries who believe His Word. We need to take hold of God and let Him take hold of us. We need to shake Heaven until we see the full fruit of our heart's desires come to pass.

CHAPTER 13

THE POWER OF THRONE
ROOM DECREES

For I want you to know, brethren, that the Gospel which was
proclaimed and made known by me is not man's gospel [a human
invention, patterned after any human standard]. For indeed I
did not receive it from man, nor was I taught it, but [it came
to me] through a [direct] revelation [given] by Jesus Christ (the
Messiah). Nor did I [even] go up to Jerusalem to those who
were apostles (special messengers of Christ) before I was, but
I went away and re- tired into Arabia, and afterward I came
back again to Damascus (Galatians 1:11-12,17).

—Paul the Apostle

Like our Father in Heaven, we have the authority to speak
Throne Room decrees by the words of our mouths. Jesus says
in Mark 11:23 that we can have what we say. In the letter to the
Hebrews (Hebrews 10:23), we are encouraged to hold fast our
confession. Once we have released our faith in the command of
faith or the prayer of faith, we must continue to believe God is
working regardless of any visible change. One of the ways we can

do this is to continue to remind God of what we are believing for by praising and thanking Him for what we trust He is doing in the unseen realm.

Upheld by His Word

There is supernatural power in the Word of God. As the Spirit unveils to us our participation in Christ, that ability is imparted to us.

> *For with God nothing is ever impossible and no word from God shall be without power or impossible of fulfillment* (Luke 1:37).

To translate this verse even more literally: no *rhema* from God shall be void of *dunamis*. In other words, when God speaks, His word carries His supernatural power. (*Rhema* is the Greek word for spoken word, *dunamis* is the Greek word for supernatural power). When we meditate in the Word, the Bible, concerning our authority, the Holy Spirit writes His laws on the tablets of our hearts. As we endure as good soldiers, we hold fast to the Word until it is manifested in the seen realm.

The words of Jesus, which were given to Him by His Father, uphold all things.

> *And He is the radiance of His glory and the exact representation of His nature, and upholds all things by the word of His power...* (Hebrews 1:3 NASB).

The Power of Speaking Throne Words

The voice of the Lord is creative power. God created everything through the power of speaking words. The voice of the Lord is a vibration that shakes and recreates the wilderness. It has the power to both create and recreate. When God speaks, we become impregnated with His word or matter. As time passes, that word grows and develops, eventually causing us to give birth to those specific promises.

However, when God's word is spoken in the realm of glory, the time it takes for the word to grow and mature is reduced to only a few moments, as time is made to serve those who know and understand their rights as citizens of Heaven. When we experience the glory of God, we experience the realm of timelessness. Just as the voice of the Lord has creative power, so too does the voice of the heirs of the Kingdom. As born-again, Spirit-filled believers, we are made in His image and, like God, hold the same position and place to speak with the voice of creative authority. This may be a stretch for some, but nonetheless is altogether true.

When we are born again, we receive with the Spirit of God all the DNA and genetics that are in Him. The God who created the seen and unseen worlds dwells inside us—this is a mystery and a beauty. The Godhead, the fullness of Deity, makes His home inside our hearts. Paul says that we should not behave as mere humans (see 1 Cor. 3:3). We are far from being mere men and women—we are possessed by Creator God.

Think about another of Paul's statements: *the Spirit of Him who raised Jesus from the dead dwells in you*" (Rom. 8:11).

What type of human being does this really make us? It makes us like God on the earth. Not that we *are* God, but we are children of God and made in His image. We are "Godlike ones." The Lord told Moses:

"See, I make you as God to Pharaoh..." (Exodus 7:1).

We speak as oracles, as God's earthly representatives. By releasing the voice of the Lord through the power of the spoken word, we can decree a thing and it will come to pass. It will happen. And it's all done by speaking words of faith.

> *You shall also decide and decree a thing, and it shall be established* for you; and the light [of God's favor] shall shine upon your ways (Job 22:28).

There are both physical and spiritual requirements for releasing the miraculous. We need the cloud of the glory of God's presence, and then we must understand how to speak into it. It's time for us to switch gears and start speaking glory-presence decrees in order to operate in the higher realities of creative miracles.

We Are the Voice of Christ

One of the greatest revelations of the New Testament is that Christ dwells within His people who live on the earth. That is why they are called the Body of Christ. We actually become the hands and feet of Jesus Christ in the earth, but we also become His mouth. God speaks prophetically through His people.

> *If anyone speaks, they should do so as one who speaks the very words of God...* (1 Peter 4:11 NIV).

Christ is the One who speaks through His people to bring salvation, healing, and deliverance. Human beings are uniquely fashioned to be the temple of God on earth. As we yield our voices to the Lord, He demonstrates His great power and extraordinary wisdom and revelation by speaking through us to the nations.

This is the ultimate unification of Heaven and earth as God unveils Christ in us and through us to the world. Our voices become the Psalm 29 sound of His voice on earth. In this way, we become an expression of the prophetic voice of the Lord. His spiritual sound is expressed through our natural sound. As we speak, He speaks through us. Mechanical sound waves become the expression of another kind of supernatural sound wave that has the capacity to penetrate the entire universe.

I've personally witnessed the reality of becoming the voice piece of the Lord as I've traveled the nations. I've watched the Lord move in union with my voice to bring about His personal directives for individuals, churches, cities, and nations with amazing power.

When the voice of the Lord speaks, I've seen, on numerous occasions, earthquakes, snowstorms, tornadoes, and hurricanes all dismantled through the power of the spoken decree. This is the sound within the sound that shakes the earth. This is the voice crying in the wilderness. In the same way that mechanical sound waves at a certain low frequency can shake a building off its foundations, so the sound waves of Heaven can shatter strongholds in our lives and bring the walls crashing down like Jericho.

We will revisit this theme in the next chapter when we explore the relationship between the prophetic proclamation of the Word of God and the release of the glory of God on earth.

Throne Room Oracles of God

We need to get ready for the new wonder workers. These new oracles of God will change cities, regions, and nations when they speak as the voice of God on the earth with the mighty word of and light that comes from the presence of the Lord. Nothing will stand before them. To date, we have seen many waves of revival hit the nations of the earth, including the United States, but nothing like we are beginning to witness now. God is propelling the maturing Body of Christ into a new place on the planet.

Miracles and power evangelism are becoming common on the streets of America and the world. A company of new oracles is rising up with the burning coals of Heaven on their lips. Like Moses, they will speak as small "g" "gods," little *elohim* creators in the earth, as "Godlike ones," declaring and decreeing the very will of God through their words. The multitudes will understand who God is as hundreds, thousands, and even millions come to Christ through demonstrations of these new wonder-working oracles of power.

We've seen some pretty remarkable things in past revivals, including the Welsh revival, The Great Awakening, Azusa Street, Latter Rain, and The Voice of Healing of the 1940s and 1950s and then later moves of God like the Toronto Blessing, Brownsville Revival, and even the much-scrutinized Lakeland Revival. Impressive as they were, they were merely "previews of the coming attraction." They will all pale in comparison to the outpouring of this new season—the outpouring of the Spirit of Revival.

The church is growing into the revelation that we really are God's representatives on this planet. And as His governmental representatives on the earth, we have been given the authority, ability, and position to function with full legal Kingdom rights to administer the job.

I can think of many events during my years of ministry where, as I came into a region, the Holy Spirit gave me something specific to say that released a sign to all who were listening. God backed up the words He gave me with incredible signs in the natural. One such event was in 2006, on the 100-year anniversary of the Azusa Street revival.

I was ministering in Topeka, Kansas, with a friend of mine, and I began to prophesy a specific word of the Lord. To confirm that this really was a Word from the Lord, I said that it would be backed up in the natural by 90-mile per hour, straight-line winds that would blow through the city, and hail would fall from the heavens. Now this was the end of March, and spring was in the air. That evening, the weather changed. On March 13, 2006, the front page of the *Topeka Capital Journal* read, "Hail in Topeka reached size of golf balls and straight-line winds reached up to ninety miles per hour."

We Speak as the Oracles of God

We are in a fresh season of global outpouring. God is unleashing something fresh that will result in churches, cities, and regions ignited in revival fire like we've never seen before. Attesting signs and wonders will follow the anointed preaching of the *rhema* Word that flows from men and women of God. We are God's mouthpieces on the planet. Peter says:

> *Whoever speaks, [let him do it as one who utters] oracles of God; whoever renders service, [let him do it] as with the strength which God furnishes abundantly, so that in all things God may be glorified through Jesus Christ (the Messiah). To Him be the glory and dominion forever and ever (through endless ages). Amen (so be it)* (1 Peter 4:11).

Oracle preaching, or *rhema* preaching under the anointing, is and always has been the standard for every generation. We speak as oracles or as God's representatives on the planet. His words are our words. By releasing the voice of the Lord through the power of the spoken word, we can decree a thing and it will come to pass. It *will* happen. People do not talk about oracles very much. To many, *oracle* is a religious word used by those interested in religion. However, oracle occurs twenty-one times in Scripture, and it carries an important meaning. So what is an oracle?

Webster's Second International Dictionary defines an oracle as, "The conduit by which God reveals hidden knowledge or makes known His divine purpose." One may recognize common words related to the word "oracle" such as oration, orator, oratory, and orison. Each finds their root in the Latin verb *orare:* to pray, utter, or speak.

An oracle is a *conduit of a message.* It is not a "medium" as in New Age spiritualists who channel demonic entities. The term here means, the package the message comes through—much like a television is a conduit of movies and news, or a pastor is a conduit of the heart of God.

CHAPTER 14

THE FIERY BAPTISM OF LOVE—INTIMACY, IDENTITY, DESTINY

Now when all the people were baptized, Jesus was also baptized, and while He was praying, heaven was opened, and the **Holy Spirit descended upon Him** *in bodily form like a dove, and a voice came out of heaven,* **"You are My beloved Son, in You I am well-pleased"** (Luke 3:21-22 NASB).

I love this passage in Luke 3, as I also love the following verse in Romans 8. When you are baptized in the Holy Spirit, you are baptized with the spirit of adoption.

For [the Spirit which] you have now received [is] not a spirit of slavery to put you once more in bondage to fear, but **you have received the Spirit of adoption** *[the Spirit producing sonship] in [the bliss of] which we cry, Abba (Father)! Father!* (Romans 8:15)

We are accepted into the family of God. No longer is God a distant force in a heavenly realm some place far away. He is our Dad, our Abba, our Papa, and our Father. He's someone we can approach with confidence, knowing that He loves us. We don't have to hide from Him because of sin—that was taken care of on the cross. We don't have to fear Him because we think He's against us, or waiting to catch us doing something bad so that He can punish us. We no longer need to have an unhealthy fear that thinks we are going to be tormented (1 John 4:18). God is for us, not against us (Rom. 8:31).

Reading Luke 3:21-22, you can clearly see that Jesus Himself was baptized in the Holy Spirit. Afterward, He was led into the desert so that He could overcome the devil. What some people fail to realize is what God meant when He says, *"You are My beloved Son, in You I am well-pleased."* I like to call this the Baptism of Love.

Take note: Jesus hadn't started His ministry yet. He hadn't cast out a demon, performed a miracle, healed a sick person, or preached a single message. Why did God say that He loved Him and that He was pleased with Him? It's simply the nature of God and the extravagance of His unconditional, uncreated, multifaceted love. God loved Jesus not because of all the awesome stuff Jesus did, but because He loved Him and was pleased in Him. Jesus was His Son. God loves His children.

Jesus was not only baptized in the Holy Spirit, but He was also baptized in the Father's love. This gave Him strength to conquer the enemy and to make it through the next forty days in the desert. In what do you find your identity? If someone was to ask you, "Who are you?" what would you say? Some might respond with their job title: "I'm a dentist." Others might reply with their calling and function in the Kingdom: "I'm an evangelist."

However, that really doesn't answer the question. That's not who you *are*. You don't find your identity in what you *do*; you find it in relationship with God. You are His child—His son or daughter. Some people find their identities in their possessions—in what they own. You can't find your identity in your belongings. You find it in to whom you *belong*. Identity is knowing *who* you are and *whose* you are.

So, who are you? The answer to the question is, "I'm a child of God." Revelation of your identity as a son or a daughter of God is birthed out of intimacy and relationship with Him. *Intimacy* releases *identity*, and *identity* releases *destiny*. Walking in a right relationship with Father God breaks off all fear and worry. How many people are plagued with worry? We tend to worry about money, food, relationships, clothes, jobs, etc. Anything that can be worried about, we don't miss the opportunity to worry. Knowing that God is your Father breaks off all that worry (see Matt. 6:25-34) and helps propel you into your destiny.

Identity Theft—Identify Releases Destiny

When Jesus was baptized in the Holy Spirit and in the Father's love, a supernatural strength was imparted into Him so He could overcome everything satan threw at Him over the next forty days in the desert.

> *Jesus, full of the Holy Spirit, returned from the Jordan and was led around by the Spirit in the wilderness for forty days, being tempted by the devil. And He ate nothing during those days...* (Luke 4:1-2 NASB).

As recorded in the Bible, satan came to Jesus three times and tried to get Him to deviate from His calling, which was to establish the Kingdom of God in the earth. We can learn several things from Jesus' forty-day desert experience; but one thing I would like to point out is that two out of the three times satan tempts Jesus, he said, *"If You are the Son of God...?"* What was satan questioning? He was questioning Jesus' identity as God's Son. One minute, Jesus is baptized in the Father's love and a loud voice from Heaven says, *"You are My beloved Son, in You I am well-pleased"* (Luke 3:22); the next minute, satan says, *"If You are the Son of God..."* (Luke 4:3,9). Satan was trying to get Jesus to second-guess His identity as the Son of God, ultimately robbing Him of His calling and destiny on the earth. Take a closer look at this account:

> *And the devil said to Him, "If You are the Son of God, tell this stone to become bread." And Jesus answered him, "It is written, 'Man shall not live on bread alone.'"*
>
> *And he led Him up and showed Him all the kingdoms of the world in a moment of time. And the devil said to Him, "I will give You all this domain and its glory; for it has been handed over to me, and I give it to whomever I wish. Therefore if You worship before me, it shall all be Yours." Jesus answered him, "It is written, 'You shall worship the Lord your God and serve Him only.'"*
>
> *And he led Him to Jerusalem and had Him stand on the pinnacle of the temple, and said to Him, "If You are the Son of God, throw Yourself down from here; for it is written, 'He will command His angels concerning You to guard You,' and, 'On their hands they will bear You up, so that You will not strike Your foot against a stone.'"*
>
> *And Jesus answered and said to him, "It is said, 'You shall not put the Lord your God to the test.'"*

When the devil had finished every temptation, he left Him until an opportune time (Luke 4:3-13 NASB).

So much of what we wrestle with in our lives is about identity. Television advertisements try to make you feel like you *absolutely need* to buy their products. One of the tactics is to attack your sense of identity. In order for you to be truly *happy* and *fulfilled,* and in order for you to be *cool* and *accepted,* you need to buy this product. The reality is that genuine fulfillment comes from the Father's love, not from worrying about your reputation or what people think.

When you sin, does the enemy come and say to you, "See, you sinner! You messed up again. God isn't going to accept you!" What about, "You're not even born again," or "You're worthless." These are all lies of the enemy that get you to question your identity as a child of God and your value and worth to Him. This is why satan is called the accuser of the brethren (Rev. 12:10); he is always pointing his finger.

When God speaks to us, it's never a voice of accusation—He doesn't make us feel guilty or condemned (Rom. 8:1). The Holy Spirit does, however, *convict* us of sin (John 16:7-8). When He speaks, it always imparts love, mercy, grace, and strength to our inner being (Eph. 3:16) so we can overcome whatever we're wrestling. His word lifts us from the pit.

Jesus entered the desert *full* of the Holy Spirit, and after forty days, He left the desert in the *power* of the Holy Spirit (Luke 4:14). There was a strengthening that happened in His identity as the Son of God when He was tempted by and overcame satan. Every time we go through a trial season and overcome, something is solidified inside us. We're not only *filled* with the Holy Spirit, but we also begin to operate in the *power* of the Holy Spirit. If we're in a season of difficulty, oftentimes a season of promotion is right around the corner. Jesus left the desert in the power of the Spirit, completely ready to start His ministry.

> *And Jesus returned to Galilee in the power of the Spirit, and news about Him spread through all the surrounding district. He began teaching in their synagogues.... And the book of the prophet Isaiah was handed to Him, And He opened the book and found the place where it was written, "The Spirit of the Lord is upon Me, because He anointed me to preach the gospel to the poor. He has sent me to proclaim release to the captives, and recovery of sight to the blind, to set free those who are oppressed, to proclaim the favorable year of the Lord." And He began to say to them, "Today this Scripture has been fulfilled in your hearing"* (Luke 4:14-15,17-19,21 NASB).

"Today this Scripture has been fulfilled in your hearing." Jesus had a destiny and a calling on the earth; He had a mission. He was commissioned into His *destiny* after solidifying His *identity*, which was birthed from *intimacy* with the Father and understanding the Father-heart of God.

> *But who can endure the day of His coming? And who can stand when He appears? For He is like a refiner's fire and like fullers' soap. He will sit as a smelter and purifier of silver, and He will purify the sons of Levi and refine them like gold and silver, so that they may present to the Lord offerings in righteousness* (Malachi 3:2-3 NASB).

We must draw close to the heart of God and allow Him to mold and shape our character. We must receive the baptism of the Father's love and let His Word wash over us. We must embrace the presence of God and lean on Him completely in those seasons of purification and purging. Why? Because when it's all through, we come out in the *power* of the Spirit, as gold refined by fire—commissioned into our Kingdom destinies that will turn the world upside down.

The Holy Spirit Will Set You Ablaze

I'd like to end with a sermon by minister and author Dr. Wesley L. Duewel. Dr. Duewel has decades of experience in missions and has authored many books about revival and the power of the Holy Spirit. His words and sentiments echo my own beliefs so well that I thought it only fitting to include them here.

The Holy Spirit Will Set You Ablaze by Wesley L. Duewel[1]

The Holy Spirit is the wonderful third Person of the Trinity about whom we know so little. He loves so tenderly, cares so personally, and ministers to us so faithfully. How amazing that perhaps the most common symbol of this beautiful Person found in the Bible is flaming fire! Why does Scripture choose fire to illustrate His presence and role? What blessedness does this suggest for us when we are Spirit-filled?

An important symbolical message for us in the fire of the Spirit is undoubtedly His work of purifying. This is the central reality in the experience of being filled with the Spirit (Acts 15:9). However, there are other significant truths taught by the fire-symbol of the Spirit. Let us look at these.

John the Baptist had prophesied of Jesus that "He will baptize you with the Holy Spirit and with fire" (Matt. 3:11; Luke 3:16). The coming of the Spirit is to have the effect of fire. Christ desired that all the fiery ministry of the Spirit be active in the life of His own. He kindled the holy flame of God in the hearts of His followers as He began His earthly ministry. Only on the day of Pentecost, as visibly symbolized by the descent of the holy flame of the Spirit, did Christ so empower by His fiery baptism that the 120 began to spread God's holy fire across the world.

Jesus had said, "I have come to bring fire on the earth" (Luke 12:49). While not all commentators are agreed as to the meaning of this fire which Christ so longed to have arrive, yet over the centuries a host of noted scholar-leaders of the Church have seen it as referring to or including reference to the mighty ministry of the Spirit.

Zeal for accomplishing God the Father's purpose was burning in Jesus like an unquenchable fire. He had a "burning readiness to do all the Father's will, even though it cost Him His blood." Our flaming-hearted Savior should have disciples with hearts similarly aflame.

Bishop William Quayle, speaking of a leader, said he "stands at the center of a circle whose entire rim is fire. Glory envelops him. He is a prisoner of majesty." He says that even the speechless should become ablaze on such themes as the Gospel compels us to grapple with. "We must not be insipid. There is not a dull page in all this age-long story of the redeeming of the race."

Quayle pleads with us not to be apathetic but to be vigilant. We "are burdened with a ministry which must be uttered lest we die, and, what is more of consequence, which must be uttered lest this wide world die." Let your heart be kindled with his further words: the minister "has his own heart strangely hot. Love girds him. The Christ applauds him. Eternity becomes his tutor. Heaven owns him as its ambassador. With him is God well pleased. A thousand points of fire leap along the horizon of his loving thought and design.

Benjamin Franklin confessed that he often went to hear George Whitefield because he could watch him burn before his very eyes. We have forgotten the root meaning from which we get our word "enthusiastic." It is from *en theos*, i.e., in God. When God gets His flaming Spirit into our personalities He naturally burns within us with holy dynamic. We become ablaze and we set others ablaze. It is a sin for a Christian leader to be drab and uninspiring.

That prince of English preachers, Dr. Martyn Lloyd-Jones, insists, "Preaching is theology coming through a man who is on fire...What is the chief end of preaching? I like to think it is this. It is to give men and women a sense of God and His presence."

A respected educator of New York University, H.H. Horne, said the secret of great teaching is contagion. This is the secret of all great leadership, of whatever kind. Martin Luther did not want to lose the fire from his soul; neither dare we. Fire attracts. Fire motivates. Fire kindles fire; it is the nature of fire to set ablaze....

God said to Jeremiah, "I will make my words in your mouth a fire" (Jer. 5:14). On that occasion God was referring to fire as a judgment. But God similarly makes our words fiery in order that His people may become aflame with holy love, zeal, and obedience.

When the Holy Spirit sets our heart aflame He will cause our words to be aflame. When our personality is aflame with commitment to Christ and with a burning vision of what He purposes to do for us, our whole leadership comes alive with life and becomes vibrant with power.

We must constantly maintain our consecration, even as the priests maintained the fire on the altar of the temple. God honors when we make repeated occasions to renew our commitment, confess our total dependence upon Him, and appropriate and implore anew His gracious Spirit's ministry within and through us. Let us note more fully this fiery ministry of the Spirit.

He sets you aflame with His fiery baptism. "He will baptize you with the Holy Spirit and with fire," said John the Baptist of Jesus (Matt. 3:11; Luke 3:16). This refers to "the fiery character of the Spirit's operations upon the soul— searching, consuming, refining, sublimating—as nearly all good interpreters understand the words." (Jamieson, Fausset, and Brown, *Commentary*, 888). The inner fire of the Spirit sets the Spirit-filled person ablaze with His divine presence.

He empowers you with His fiery divine energy. The fire of God speaks also of His divine energy constantly ready to empower His own who are totally surrendered to Him. Christ desires that all the fiery ministry of the Spirit be active in your life. "I have come to bring fire on the earth" (Luke 12:49). He kindled the holy flame of God in the hearts of His followers as He began His earthly ministry. But He knew they needed more of the Spirit.

On the day of Pentecost, the Holy Spirit visibly descended in holy flame upon the men and women gathered in the Upper Room. Empowered by the Spirit, they began to spread God's holy fire that very day. For decades the Spirit's fire kept burning and spreading. Persecution could not quench their fire, it only served to fan the flames. Pentecost lit a flame that by God's grace will never go out.

He sets you aglow with His fiery radiance and zeal. Romans 12:11 urges, "Never be lacking in zeal, but keep your spiritual fervor." You have spiritual zeal when you are spiritually ablaze. Weymouth translates this, "Have your spirits aglow"; Goodspeed, "on fire with the Spirit"; and the Revised Standard Version states it, "Be aglow with the Spirit."

The Holy Spirit revives your spirit, fills you with abundance of life, love and zeal, and sets you aglow so that you manifest the vibrant, radiant life of God. He will revive your devotion, accelerate your obedience, and fan into fame your zeal. As a Spirit-filled believer you should be marked by the intense devotion, eager earnestness, and the loyal bond-service, which characterizes the heavenly angels. Apollos (Acts 18:25) was thus ablaze. The literal translation can be that he was "burning in spirit," or "glowing with the Spirit."

When the Spirit burns within you in freedom and fullness, your inner life becomes radiant, your zeal intense, and your service dynamic. You, in the words of Ephesians 5:16, are "making the most of every opportunity."

The need for this spiritual glow and zeal is emphasized by the condition of the church in Laodicea, which had grown lukewarm (Rev. 3:15-16). The spiritual temperature of a Spirit-filled leader should remain high. The Spirit desires so to fill you with burning, glowing agape love that your life is constantly radiant with His presence. Whether the translation of Romans 12:11 is to be aglow with the Holy Spirit or to be aglow in your own spirit, the Enabler is ever the Spirit Himself. His active fullness must permeate your personality and service.

He provides you gifts which you are to stir into flame. Spiritual gifts are endowments for service given through the activity of the Holy Spirit. God provides whatever divine enablements we need for the service to which He appoints us. The Holy Spirit Himself is God's great gift to us (Acts 2:38) but He bestows grace-gifts (charismata) providing divine endowment and enablement for serving God and the Body of Christ.

"Fan into flame the gift of God which is in you," Paul urged Timothy (2 Tim. 1:6). Notice the gift was "in" him. The Holy Spirit primarily works from within, not upon in some external sense. He does not manipulate us, He enables by His indwelling presence and power.

God never appoints or guides you to do a service without being available to endow and empower you with all you need to do His will. But there is a cooperating role for you to play. You must kindle anew, or fan into full flame the divine endowment. God's gifts are given to be cherished and used. To fail to use them as God desires is to fail God and people. We develop them by use. As we use God's endowment, the Spirit enables us, guides us, and makes us fruitful.

The constant tendency of fire is to go out. The Spirit does not waste divine energy. If we do not obey and use the grace God provides, He ceases to bestow. The Greek tense of the verb emphasizes the continuous rekindling of the flame. The spiritual biography of many a Christian leader is "once ablaze." Was there a time when you were more ablaze for God than you are today?

Praise God, a flickering flame that is almost gone can be fanned into brilliant fire again. That fanning must be a continuous process. Five times in Leviticus 6 God instructed that the fire on the altar of burnt offering was never to go out. He had initially given that fire from heaven (Lev. 9:24; 2 Chron. 7:11). God supplies the fire, but we must keep it burning. We constantly need the Spirit's fire, symbolizing the divine presence within us, and we constantly need the touch of God's grace provided through the atonement upon us. Our consecration to God should never lapse and His presence and power in and upon us should never diminish.

God has created our spirits flammable. We are spiritually combustible. Our nature is created to be set ablaze by the Spirit. We are spiritually most blessed, most victorious, most usable when we are ablaze. We are most Godlike when we glow with holy flame—the flame of the indwelling Spirit.

The fire of God gives an unforgettable attraction to the personality of God's messenger and to the content of his message. It imparts a sacred authority that cannot be counterfeited by human efforts. It so seals with the mark of God that others are unable to ignore it. It gives a holy authenticity and assures of integrity. It impresses with the obvious involvement and partnership of God.

Whatever the cost, we must keep the flame of the Spirit burning on the altar of our hearts. The Greek word in "fan into flame" in Second Timothy 1:6 refers to the use of a bellows to cause a smoldering fire to flame up. This takes effort. Timothy was to do all in his power to intensify the manifestation of the flame of the Spirit. Our cooperation with the Spirit is essential to consistency of flowing ardor, spiritual radiance, and flaming zeal.

General Booth urged his people, "The tendency of fire is to go out; watch the fire on the altar of your heart." Our constant danger is to cool off spiritually, to lose our fervor, and to slow down in zeal. Personal revival comes through renewed commitment and reaffirmed consecration. Everyone needs such personal revival again and again.

We have the great gift of God, the Holy Spirit, but we need to hunger more for the manifestation of His presence, and open our hearts constantly in faith's expectancy for His working, His empowerings and constant enablings in our life. God gives us capacity and the Spirit wants to imbue our whole being with His reality, making us His channels of expression that His holy fire may be constantly visible in us. We must choose whether we will neglect the Spirit, quench the Spirit, or fan into flame the Spirit's presence.

Endnote

1. Wesley L. Duewel, "The Holy Spirit Will Set You Ablaze," sermonindex.net; http://www.sermonindex.net/modules/articles/index.php?view=article&aid=27950; accessed December 20, 2017.

ABOUT THE AUTHOR

Jeff Jansen is an internationally known conference speaker and crusade evangelist. Jeff is also the Founder of Global Fire Ministries International, and Senior Pastor of the Global Fire Church and World Miracle Center located in Murfreesboro, Tennessee.

These ministries include:

- Global Fire Church & World Miracle Center
- Global Fire TV
- Global Fire International Crusades
- Global Fire Covenant Network (A Fellowship of Church)
- Global Fire Prayer Furnace (10 state Regional Revival Meetings)

Jeff's burning desire is to see churches, cities, regions, and whole nations ignited and transformed by the power of God. Jeff flows in a strong prophetic and miracle healing anointing that releases the tangible glory of God everywhere he goes. Jeff also teaches, trains, and equips believers how to live and move in the supernatural presence of God and emphasizes that communion and intimacy with the Holy Spirit is vital for transformation.

Jeff believes that the same Holy Spirit that rested in and upon Jesus Christ then is the same Spirit that flows in and through the corporate Body of Christ now, and that we are to be equipped and released as Kingdom ambassadors to the nations of the earth.

Global Fire Ministries in an interdenominational ministry aimed at equipping and igniting the Body of Christ for Global harvest.

Jeff, his wife, Jan, and family live in the Nashville, Tennessee, area.

CONTACT INFORMATION

Global Fire Ministries
325 Walla Court
Murfreesboro, TN 37128
Website: www.globalfireministries.com
Email: info@globalfireministries.com
Twitter: @jeff_jansen
Facebook.com/JeffJansenFanPage/

**GLOBAL
FIRE
CREATIONS**

Visit our website at: www.globalfirecreations.com

RECEIVE A FREE GIFT Subscribe to our e-newsletter and
receive a free downloadable gift
visit: www.globalfireministries.com to subscribe

To Purchase Additional **Global Fire Creations** Products

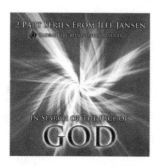

visit: www.globalfirestore.com

ALSO AVAILABLE from the Global Fire Store:

In Search of the Face of God
2 CD Teaching Series

The Sound of Glory: Soaking CD
by Jeff Jansen and Julian & Melissa Wiggins

These and many more faith-building and encouraging products are available from www.globalfirestore.com.

OTHER BOOKS BY JEFF JANSEN

Glory Rising, Glory Rising Manual

Adventures in the Prophetic

School of the Holy Spirit

The Believer's Guide to Miracles, Healing, Impartation & Activation

Revival of the Secret Place